OAKWOOD
MEMORIES

Compiled by

Jeanne Bennett Calvert

for the

Oakwood Library Association

2013

ISBN-13: 978-0615936932
ISBN-10: 0615936938

Quail Hollow Press
6916 State Route 66
Oakwood, Ohio 45873
skydancr@tds.net

A Brief History of Oakwood

Wilford V. Kretzinger prepared this article for the Oakwood News.

From Everett's A. Budd's History of Paulding County:

"Oakwood was laid out as a village, September 17, 1872, by William C. Hedges and the surveying done by L. E. Holtz of Ottawa. As early, however as 1851, goods were sold by John Crossen who owned the farm upon which most of the village stands. In 1854, when the Tiffen and Ft. Wayne railroad (Now Nickel Plate) was being built, a general store was opened by a contractor named Hazzen and run until the road collapsed. Shortly after the (Civil) War S.S. Shisler and N. C. Whiting opened small country stores in the place and Mr. Whiting established a ferry for the transportation of teams and passengers across the Auglaize. A post office was established some years before the town was laid out, on a mail route leading from Ottawa to Charloe. This route was maintained until the opening of the Nickel Plate in 1881. The place received a boom in 1871-72 while the "Continental Railway" was in the process of construction, but it was not until some ten years later, on the completion of the New York, Chicago, St. Louis and Pacific Railway, that it began to show signs of permanent thrift, upon which has been built a prosperous and enterprising village."

A grist mill, three stories was built at the corner of First and Walnut Streets in 1886 by Leonard Zimmerman and was operated until about 1908. It was torn down in 1918. A steam engine furnished the power to operate the mill.

The first tile mill in use for several years was followed by a second one built at the east side of town. The latter burned down in July 1913.

There was a hoop and stave mill located at the east side of town during its early history but it was moved away when timber became scarce.

A saw and planing mill was owned and operated by Cy Hoover quite a number of years. It was located on the south side of the railroad between First and Second Streets. It has been gone some fifty years.

Oakwood had a lime kiln for a time sixty-five years ago (about 1890), it being located on the east bank of the Auglaize near the road bridge. It was reported that the lime produced was not of the best quality.

Oakwood has had only one railroad, the Nickel Plate. It was in process of construction for nearly thirty years under different names, but was finally completed as the Nickel Plate early in 1882. When the road was constructed, First Street of Oakwood crossed over it by a steep grade. About sixty years ago (1895 +/-) the underpass was built.

The viaduct photographed by Dean Lighthill
Notice the street is unpaved.

The first school building, a two story, two room brick building was erected in 1884. Some fifteen years later, two more rooms were added. In 1918-19, this building was torn down and a new and more modern building constructed at a cost of about $30,000. Since that time two additions have been added costing around $180,000. Some of the school's superintendents have been E. S. Cummings, Logan Snook, L. M. Eschbach, S. C. Coil, L. F. Chalfant, Mr. Hanawalt, Mr. Hutchinson, Tom Ritchie, Miss Helen Gillespie, O. O. Gardner, Mr. Barr, J. M. Reed, Mr. Ryder, P. D. Koeppe, R.C. Neiswander, Emery J. Kretzinger and C. R. Estle, the present superintendent.

The first school building

The M. E. Church has been active since the early history of Oakwood, the church building being first located on the south side of the railroad at the corner of Walnut and Second Streets. A new building was later built at the corner of Harmon & Second streets and is still in use. It has been remodeled a couple of times since the original construction.

The Methodist Evangelical Church as it originally looked.

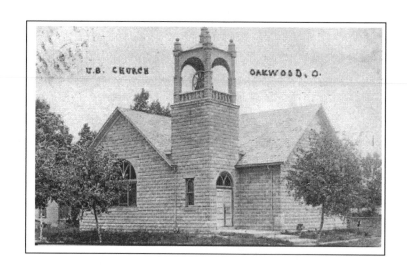

The United Brethren Church built in 1909

The U. B. Church (now E. U. B.) had its beginning in Oakwood in 1897, occupying the same location as formerly occupied by the M. E. Church. The Disciples of Christ also used this building for a time prior to its purchase by the U. B. Church. In 1909, the U. B. Church sold this building and constructed a cement block building at the corner of Main and Second Streets. It has been remodeled and transformed into a frame building with basement.

From the Oakwood News 1955

In about 1877, the first stationary engine and boiler was loaded on flatboat by Si Hoover, slid down the bank on the Burr Lighthill farm (near where the Shisler mink farm was located) and floated down the river to Oakwood. It was taken out of the river and placed where Jacobs bee house later stood. Some of the men who worked in the mill operated by this engine were: Simon Matson, Eliat Matson, Charles Matson and George Whiting. They processed lumber for flooring and siding.

In about 1882, a steamboat operated on the Auglaize and lower part of the Blanchard River. Mr. Bridleman built the boat at the stave mill which he operated just north of the railroad bridge. He towed flat boats with his steamboat, unloading for Dupont near the County Line Bridge. He went as far south as S. Mt. Zion Church on the Blanchard.

In 1883, the church called The Oak Grove Church, also known as the Old German Baptist Church was organized near the County Line Bridge. Henry Prowant was the first minister. The church is gone but the cemetery remains.

In 1956, the old mill pond one the west side of Sixth Street was filled in and the area "bulldozed" smooth.

In 1956, Virg and Ralph Cooper had one of the largest goose farms in Northwestern Ohio. It is located on the former Eakins farm near Blue Creek. They have 550 older geese that produce eggs. After hatching, the goslings are shipped to every state east of the Rocky Mountains.

In 1956, a farm just south of Oakwood sold for $262.50 an acre. It was purchased by Alvin Maddock.

On January 12, 1918, the temperature was between 15 and 22 below zero in Oakwood. The roads were blocked with snow and there were no snowplows available to clear them. Some places the snow on the highways was four feet deep. Men from town took shovels, the following week and tried to open up some entrances to the village. Snow along the pathways they made was higher than a horse's back. There were so many below-zero days in January that year that people began to say, "it was only zero this morning" and "it sure feels good to have it moderate like this."

The Auglaize River

As I approach my 80th birthday, I find myself recalling things that happened many years ago. It seems strange that I can remember such things when sometimes I can't recall my Social Security or telephone number. The good news is that I'm not alone in this. If you're past 60, you can relate. The way I see it, if we can re-live the good memories and screen out the bad, life is great. I've been thinking lately about the

Auglaize River and how it has affected my life. When I was a kid, we lived on a farm two miles north of Oakwood. And I still do. The river runs right through the village. And by cutting across the fields, we could reach our best fishing spot.

We would usually go back to Bub Shisler's woods or down behind the George Specht farm.

At this point, I guess I should alert you to look out for the Yogis in my ramblings. Yogi Berra, the longtime catcher for the New York Yankees, once said. "When you come to a fork in the road, take it!" So when I change directions unexpectedly, and you get a little bit lost, we'll just call it a Yogi.

Floyd Burt, who operated the Shell Station in Oakwood, had a female rat terrier. She was the best rat-killing dog anyone had ever seen. So when she had pups, they were in great demand. This was, of course, before we had rat poison. So shooting and trapping the pests were the only other alternatives. Several of the families in the area... the Adamses, the Grimes and the Carnahans... got pups from that great dog and on occasion they'd go on rat-killing excursions. One of my fishing buddies was Jerry Carnahan, who lived right on Route 66 south of us... right where the Rhino Lining facility now sits. One day, when I was heading for the river, I stopped to get Jerry. The rat hunters were gathering there when we left. Laurel Carnahan... Jerry's dad... had a small corn crib attached to a machine shed. Most of the ear corn had been used out of it and it was crawling with rats. When we returned from fishing, we saw that the fellas had killed a huge number of rats and piled them up in the driveway. I wish I had a photo of that pile to share with you. But of course, I do have one in my mind's eye and I can make it any size I so choose.

I had an experience when I was in about the sixth grade that's not the least bit cloudy in my mind. We had on our farm a 10 by 30 foot silo. And when it was empty, we'd store its wooden doors around the inside of its cement edge until fall. That year, I was given the task of cleaning the dirt off the silo floor in preparation for filling. Most of that dirt was the dropping from the monkey faced owls who made their nests in the top of the silo. The droppings contained hundreds of skeleton parts from mice and other creatures that the owls had lived on during the summer. My attire was a pair of tan bib overalls that were too big for me as usual.

You see, Mom would usually buy clothes for me that were a bit too big and just say, "Oh, Billy, you'll grow into 'em." I mention this because, while I was moving one of the silo doors so I could clean the floor under it, a big brown rat ran out from under it, up my overalls leg and out the top of my shirt. Oh! OH!! I can STILL feel that rascal crawling! I guess we just had a Yogi.

So I'll go back to my river thoughts. There was a large island near the spot where Jerry and I liked to fish and most of the time there was a small boat tied up there. One time we decided to row out and fish off the island. But as we were docking our boat, two big, black water snakes slithered down the bank. We made a hasty retreat and chose a different place. Many times there would be a man there who lived nearby and he could beat the pants off me when it came to fishing. I could sit right beside him, use the same bait and he'd catch fish and I'd hardly get a nibble. He'd say, "Billy, you're not holding your pole right." His name was Sam Fuller and he and his wife Annie were wallpaper hangers, which they did way past the time when Sam's eyes got weak. They papered my bedroom one time. For Christmas the year before, I'd received a model kit of the plane Charles Lindbergh had flown across the Atlantic. And I was proudly displaying it by hanging it from a tack in the middle of my ceiling. When we were preparing the room, we took all the pictures and other things down, but we forgot to pull that tack. Sure enough, Sam proceeded to paper right over it, leaving a raised area about as big as a saucer. Oh, well. Who was going to check my ceiling anyway?

The Auglaize River also caused me to get the one and only F I ever got on my grade card. In the winter of '43 – '44, the river was frozen hard and it remained frozen for several weeks. I remember that Bert Bradford from Continental had made an ice boat, with a sail and all. Well, it was almost time for exams in school and Maude Chase, my home-room teacher, told us the day before that if we finished our exams early, we could go to the river and skate. So it was that Bill Bidlack finished very early and got an F on his arithmetic exam – brought down by the hand of Mother Nature.

The river was pretty clear at that time, since there were no cesspools draining into it. The worst pollution we'd get was when somebody at the sugar beet factory in Ottawa accidently released water from its settling ponds and killed fish for several miles downstream.

The biggest flood Oakwood ever suffered was in 1913. My father, Lawrence Bidlack, was the cashier at the Oakwood Deposit Bank at the time and he and mother lived in the house that Dr. Leatherman later lived in for so long. Mother was very pregnant with my sister Mabel at the time. And it seems she and Dad waited a little too long before heading for higher ground and Mom finally rode away in a rowboat. The most recent real flood that I can recall... there have been many lesser ones... was in 1952 when the water got just about clear down Main Street ... Route 66. At that time, Mick Huff operated the Huff and Puff Restaurant and the water got clear up to the second step of his entrance. I recall the incident so well because Mick was on a bowling team with four others from the area ... John Leatherman, Bill Wagner, Todd Roughton, and I ... and we were supposed to bowl in a Legion tournament that weekend but had to scratch.

Actually, Oakwood is very much like a lot of other small towns in the area ... struggling to stay afloat. However, we're filled with memories of the mighty Auglaize.

Bill Bidlack

Writing for Farmland News, June 2011

The Auglaize Valley Game Club

This group was active in Oakwood in the 1950's. They had a membership of over fifty area men. Their first club house was a wooden frame building located ¾'s of a mile east of Oakwood. In the mid 1950's they moved to a building that they erected in Shisler's woods near the skating rink north of town.

They were involved in many community activities, donated items for the town park and released hundreds of young peasants in the area.

The Baseball Park

The Oakwood Booster Association was formed in 1956 with the purpose of having a lighted baseball park in Oakwood. Six directors were selected: Dick Donley, president, Virgil Colwell, vice president, Todd Roughton, secretary-treasurer, Dale Roughton, Wayne Miller and Dan Dodge. Membership in the organization costs $1.00.

Shortly after formation, the association purchased 30 used flood lights for $200. Scott and Hazel Badman donated a site on the east end of town and Badman Field was born.

1941 Basketball Team

Come along with me as we travel back to the 1940s and recall that special week of county basketball tournament time. Oakwood had several winners during the 1930s and '40s. We will center in on the 1941 team, but first a mention of something about the game.

The game of basketball has changed a lot over the years. For brevity, let's start with the center jump. Not only did the game start with a center jump, the game continued after a basket with a center jump. Having a big center gave your team an advantage. After 1937 or '38, play continued with the team scored upon inbounding the ball.

During the '30s and 40's, several trophies were won by Oakwood. Some of the stars of the 1930's were Paul Shisler, Bob McClure and Art Kimmel.

The county tournament was more than just basketball. School pride and bragging rights were on the line. Each of the 88 Ohio counties had teams playing to see who could advance to a district tournament. Win the district, and you were on your way to Columbus for the state tournament. If a county had more than six teams, both the winner and runner-up could advance to the district.

Paulding County had teams from Antwerp, Payne, Grover Hill, Latty, Haviland and Oakwood. One year Melrose entered a team so Paulding County sent two teams to the district, which was played at Leipsic. All county champs and runners-up had to play at Leipsic and win in order to make the trip to Columbus. To say the least, that was tough to do.

Paulding was an exempted village school, so they played in a different tournament.

The 1940-41 school year was memorable for the Oakwood Green Devils – later the Bobcats – in several ways. Not only were they league champs, they were county champs also.

The year started with the introduction of a new coach. Casimer Newdome, who had been coaching at Latty, was at the helm. He had been a big football star at Ohio Northern.

The Green Devils had a stellar line up. Harold Mead was at center, Walt Harris and Vic Dunlap were the forwards and Keith Matson and Rich Harris were the guards. John D. Williams, Bud Noggle, Don Burt and Junior Rickner came in as needed. Walt Harris was the team captain and did a great job leading the team.

The Green Devils opened the '41 season by defeating Latty, Mark Center and Grover Hill in the month of November. They lost to Ottawa Public.

December found the Devils beating Continental, Farmer, Ney and Haviland. They lost to Hoagland, Jackson and Paulding.

During the month of January, they beat Paulding, Antwerp, Latty, alumni, Haviland, Payne, Grover Hill and Payne. They lost to Continental and Antwerp.

A notable game was Mark Center, coached by Bill Rex and featuring future Ohio State star Max Gecowitz.

Payne was another thriller that saw Rich Harris hitting a long set shot to tie the game and then sinking two foul shots to win in overtime and the league title.

Now, it's tournament time. Antwerp and Oakwood were equally favored to take home the trophy. They split wins during the year.

Oakwood drew Latty and had little trouble beating them 55 – 23. The next game was against Grover Hill. Grover Hill, known as "The Mound City Boys," put up a good fight, but went down to defeat, 43-31.

Now it was time for the big one. Whoever won this one was county champs and on their way to Leipsic. Antwerp was sure they were going to be victorious. They had several huge piles of firewood along Main Street ready to light after returning home with the trophy. They forgot one thing. They were playing the Green Devils from Oakwood, who were the league champs.

Oakwood drew first blood and the game stayed close with Oakwood maintaining a small lead. About midway through the third quarter, Walt Harris hit two long set shots and the rout was on. Matson put in a lay-up. Rich Harris hit a long set shot off the backboard. Mead put in a lay-up and Antwerp folded.

The final score was 50-37. It was a sad dark night in Antwerp but the Devils danced the streets in Oakwood.

The district tournament was loaded with good teams. Oakwood drew Malinta from Henry County. The first half ended with Malinta leading, 26-25. The second half found Malinta playing roughhouse basketball. Oakwood could not take the punishment and went down to defeat, 48-32.

Oakwood had a great year, winning 19, losing five, hauling in the county championship and being crowned league champs.

Many long hard battles were fought on the hardwood courts that year, but a bigger and more dangerous battle front was in full swing. Many of the players would be called to serve in America's armed forces. World War II was heating up.

In a few years, Hitler and Japan would be defeated; the county tournament would be phased out. All teams would be assigned to sectionals with the winners advancing to the districts and then to regionals and then to state.

County tournament time was a special time for both adults and students. Time would change many things but the memories from this special time would always remain.

Richard Harris

Writing in the Paulding county Progress June 2011

G. Alaska and Ida (Monroe) Bennett

My grandparents G. Alaska and Ida moved to the Oakwood area in 1910, shortly after their marriage in Montezuma, Mercer County, Ohio. My grandfather and one of his brothers had purchased an 80 acre farm south of Oakwood in 1908. At that time, Alaska was a school teacher but wanted to become a farmer like his father.

Soon after their marriage in the spring, Alaska and Ida packed their belongings and headed north. They had a team of horses, a wagon, a buggy which they pulled behind the wagon and a cow which walked behind the buggy. All of their furniture, clothes, and housewares were on the wagon and in the buggy. Also they brought seedlings which Ida had started for the garden which would be one of the main priorities as soon as they arrived.

Because they could only travel as fast as their cow could walk, the journey was a slow one. They had to travel about 52 miles, a trip that today takes a little over an hour by car. It took them the best part of three days to make the trip. The two nights they were traveling, they stopped at farmhouses and asked if they could purchase lodging and food for themselves and their animals. No one turned them down.

I have often thought how much nerve it must have taken for them to start on their journey. They knew no one at the place that was going to be their home and had no idea when they would be able to see their families again.

Front: Homer, Alaska, Ida, Edgar Rear: Doris, Lois, Rex, Dorthy

The house they moved into was a log cabin. I can only imagine how busy their lives must have been as they farmed the land and made a home for themselves and their family. During the next eleven years, they were blessed with six children: three sons and three daughters: Rex who married Avis Shisler, Doris who married Aaron Kohart, Edgar who married Elsie Weaver and Aletha Gunderman, Lois, Homer who married Grace Westenbarger and Dorthy who married Horace France.

Jeanne Bennett Calvert

Cleo Durham Bidlack

Cleo was born on September 2, 1905 in Henry County to Guy Eugene and Iva (Frederick) Durham. Growing up in rural Henry County with her brothers Laverne and Burdette was a happy time for Cleo. When she was 13, her father bought a farm in Paulding County and the family moved. She did not attend school that year (1918) because of the terrible flu epidemic. The following year she attended Buntsville School, a one-room school with all eight grades. That school was within walking distance of her home. At the start of her freshman year at the new Oakwood High School, her father gave her a horse that she named Ol' Dynamite to ride the six miles to town. Her parents made special arrangements for her to live in Oakwood with a friend Jennie May, so that she could participate in the school play and other activities. She enjoyed that because Oakwood had electricity and her parents living in the country did not.

In 1924, Cleo graduated from high school and "noticed a very handsome football player named Guy Bidlack" who had graduated the year before. They dated, fell in love and married two years later. They settled down on the Bidlack farm. Since it was spring, planting took precedence over a honeymoon. They became the parents of three children: Marjorie, Don and Duane.

Cleo was a typical homemaker of the time: sewing for her children, doing the laundry on a wash board in a large copper tub and doing the ironing with irons heated on a big wood burning cook stove. In addition to housework, she also tended a big garden, canning fruits and vegetables for winter meals.

Cleo was a Sunday School teacher and made noodles and angel food cakes from many church socials and suppers. Her cooking skills got a real workout when the thrashing ring came to their house. At that time, farmers cut wheat and oats with a machine called a binder. The grain was then shocked into bundles to be thrashed. The thrashing machines were pulled by teams of horses and the neighbors formed thrashing rings to accomplish this task. When it was time for the thrashers to come to the house, the neighbor women helped cook the meals.

They would cook roast beef, real mashed potatoes, gravy, homemade noodles and all kinds of vegetables from the garden, salads, pies, cakes and lemonade – all without the aid of electricity.

Large tubs of warm water (taken from the reservoir kitchen stove) soap and towels were placed out in the yard for the men to wash up before eating. Even though they had a large dining room, the meal had to be served in two shifts and when the men were finished, the women and children would eat. At the end of the day after everyone went home, Guy and Cleo still had the cows to milk, the hogs, sheep and chickens to feed and the eggs to gather and of course the house to clean.

In the winter, the neighborhood ladies would gather for quilting bees to pass the time while the men did the butchering. This was another example of neighbors helping neighbors.

Cleo Bidlack

As there was no electricity in the county (they used kerosene lamps and heated the house with a wood burning stove), Guy began talking with friends and neighbors about the possibility of bringing electricity to the rural areas around Oakwood. Eventually, the Paulding Putnam Electric Co-op was form and in 1938, electricity came to their home and to those of their neighbors. Guy served on the board of the Co-op for many years.

In 1976, Guy and Cleo celebrated their golden wedding anniversary and were honored as Mr. and Mrs. Oakwood. Guy died the next year of heart failure. Cleo continued to live in the family home for many years, eventually moving in with her daughter and later living at the Laurels of Defiance. In 2005, she celebrated her 100th birthday. She passed away on October 31, 2008.

Based on an article in the Crescent News October 2005

Frances Bidlack Heidenescher remembers

When I was a small child at Grandma Hulda Bidlack's, they must have been burning the ditch, but I remember someone kicking over a burnt hen and there were little chicks under her that were still alive.
Now I remember this verse and understand how God wants us close to him so he can protect us.
Luke 13:34
"O Jerusalem, Jerusalem, which killest the prophets, and stonest them that are sent unto thee; how often would I have gathered thy children together, as a hen doth gather her brood under her wings, and ye would not!"

I was taught to memorize scriptures from an early age. One my mother used to tell us was:
 Numbers 32:23 b "... and be sure your sin will find you out."

Being raised in a small town, somehow Momma always found out what I did.
And one time as a teenager my older brother Orville heard I was drunk and falling in a ditch. The "talking to" he gave me I'll never forget. I had drank a beer, but while I was walking with a friend to her home after skating, she wet her pants laughing, and some boys were following us in their car. She had on a short coat and I had on a long one. She asked me to squat down and change coats with her before they noticed she was wet.
1 Thessalonians 5:22
"Abstain from all appearance of evil." Is another verse that brings back many memories of days gone by. I'm 70 year old now and not capable

of "much evil" any more, but I still need to guard against it. Especially since there is so much evil around us in our current world.

Blowing up the Oakwood Jail

The Oakwood Jail was blown up, I believe in the winter of 1905. O. S. Ritchie was mayor at the time. Lafe Fisher was living over by the depot and had a bar in his front room. He kept it open on Sundays and Ritchie had him arrested and sentenced him to 10 days in the Oakwood Jail. Fisher refused to go to jail until it was cleaned up and sanitary.

Here's what happened: the night before, someone took dynamite and fuses from Martin Bidlack's Hardware Store, located in the old Yutsy Building. They left the money in the store after taking six pounds of the explosive and 50 feet of fuse and caps. This was placed under the jail about midnight and set off. It tore the jail into pieces and set the bunk on top of a nearby roof.

Right off the "bat" the mayor suspicioned Charles Bobenmyer and Oscar Randolph. We both were arrested and tried in Paulding and were acquitted. They never did find out who "pulled" the job. Fisher later served the 10 days in the county jail in Paulding.

The story doesn't end here: it goes on like this: Sank French was the correspondent for the Chicago American newspaper at the time and it came out with the whole front page carrying the story of how the Oakwood Jail was blown up, stating that 14 people were in the jail at the time, and of course this raised a lot of excitement all over the country.

Charles Bobenmyer
In a letter published in the Oakwood News

Loy and Wilma Boroff

Working at the Oakwood Post Office in 1985 I met Loy Boroff. Loy was a retired railroad man. Every day Loy would come to the post office to pick up his mail and chat. You see despite our age difference we had a lot in common. Loy collected stamps and I really loved stamps too. Loy was also an awesome gardener and we talked garden more times than I can count. I don't think I ever met Loy's wife Wilma until Loy got very ill and was in the hospital. While putting mail into the boxes I saw their box open. I ran out to meet her and ask about my friend Loy. So began my friendship with Wilma. Loy was always sharing plants and seeds and I was never allowed to say thank you because that caused a plant not to grow according to Loy. I still have some of the seeds in bottles that Loy gave me. Maybe they would still grow but I just keep the bottles with the seed names written in his hand writing and some old seeds in his memory. Every spring when I dig into my gardening stuff there are my seeds and there are my memories.

I wrote a story about Loy a few years ago called Loy's Cookies. I wrote about the Christmas cookies I baked and had been sharing with over 25 of my family and friends. One year I decided the cost was too much and my back was too sore so I wasn't going to bake. Along came Loy who said, "Me and Wilma can't wait for those cookies, have you got them all baked yet?" No way could I tell this nice old guy I wasn't baking this year. So I went home and I baked, not as much as usual but I baked for my friends who I knew could not bake anymore. I never told Loy but those were probably the best cookies I ever made because I baked them especially for him. I made sure I baked his favorites and I remember standing in the kitchen and being happy because I knew he loved cookies.

After Loy passed, I began my friendship with Wilma. You know she wasn't the gardener or stamp collector that Loy was but we found plenty to talk about. Loy and Wilma Boroff are some of the best people I have ever known. I still get a little sad when I drive by their old house and look out and think of the times I stopped by to see Loy's garden or flowers.

By Shelly Roughton

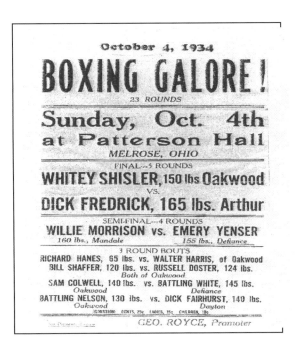

October 4, 1934

BOXING GALORE!
23 ROUNDS

Sunday, Oct. 4th
at Patterson Hall
MELROSE, OHIO

FINAL—5 ROUNDS

WHITEY SHISLER, 150 lbs Oakwood
vs.
DICK FREDRICK, 165 lbs. Arthur

SEMI-FINAL—4 ROUNDS

WILLIE MORRISON vs. EMERY YENSER
160 lbs., Mandale   155 lbs., Defiance

3 ROUND BOUTS

RICHARD HANES, 65 lbs. vs. WALTER HARRIS, of Oakwood
BILL SHAFFER, 120 lbs. vs. RUSSELL DOSTER, 124 lbs.
Both of Oakwood
SAM COLWELL, 140 lbs. vs. BATTLING WHITE, 145 lbs.
Oakwood   Defiance
BATTLING NELSON, 130 lbs. vs. DICK FAIRHURST, 140 lbs.
Oakwood   Dayton
ADMISSION: GENTS, 25c   LADIES, 15c   CHILDREN, 10c

GEO. ROYCE, Promoter

Boxing

Boxing was local entertainment that often was held in Oakwood and surrounding communities. This bill is from 1934 and most of the participants had local connections. "Whitey" Shisler was Harley Shisler. His son Nolan said his father received $2.50 for participating in the Main Event.

The Richard Hanes listed was really Richard Harris. The promoter did not want people to realize that the two contenders were brothers. After their fight, Walter told Harley that he and Richard made more than Harley because people threw dimes and nickels into the ring and he and Richard divided this extra "pay".

After Lester Shisler built the Wood U Drive Inn Skating Rink in the mid 1950's, he built an amphitheater in the woods north of the rink and boxing and wrestling matches were held there. A 116 foot long wooden foot bridge was built to allow visitors to reach the amphitheater.

Karen Ort Bradford remembers the beauty shop, card club and more

On November 19, 1988, Larry and I got married in Woodburn, Indiana. Soon after that we bought "Country Clip and Curl" from Sue Kesler. Buying the shop was a good choice. I met lots of people, heard lots of stories, lots of jokes, and people shared lots of memories and shared sadness which comes with life.

The jokes came about every Friday morning. Friday morning always started with the Oakwood telephone ladies, Pat Northcutt and Sheila Gardner. Those two were pretty well behaved when you see who came in next. The beauticians would come in: Tami Dobbelaere, Lydia Ferris, Becky Jo Thomas and myself. Our clients on Friday mornings usually were Betty Tanner, Norma Spencer, Pauline Cooper, Mary Bidlack, Mary Lou Porter, Dorothy Merritt, Viola Dobbelaere, and Wanda Bennett. That is just a few of the ones that came in in the A.M. If you knew them, you can imagine the stories they could tell. Then in the afternoon we would have Wanda Miller, Helen Varner Thomas, Velma Keck, Vernel Baker, Rosemary Thomas and the fun would begin again.

As time went on, we lost our clients, they grew old and some passed away, some went into nursing homes or assisted living. In later years, I went to work at Country Inn Enhanced Living Center. Velma Keck came there to live, soon Helen Thomas, Pauline Cooper and there I met Eleanor Justinger, also from Oakwood. They have all passed on but I have such good memories of them

My mother in law, Donnabelle Bradford always had lunch at 11:30; somehow no matter who stopped in she always had enough food for everyone. I still do not know how she managed that. My father in law always watched "Mayberry" after lunch usually holding at least one great grandchild on his lap. After Bernard passed away, we do not think Donnabelle ever cooked. She would be at the "Iron Skillet – now Phil's Diner" every day sitting in the booth in front of the windows. Many children came to know her as "Grandma B."

Several of us had a card club for many years. Dianne Cooper, Jeanne Calvert, Paula Thomas, Becky Jo Thomas, Athena Brown, Sharon Peck, Joyce Estle, Carolyn Roughton, Joanne Fitzwater, Lydia Ferris Sharon Sierer, and the late Erm Weller and Marlene Thompson. I never figured out if we liked to play cards, eat or gossip or all of the above but we always had a good time.

I gained two great stepchildren: Tina Fitzwater and her husband Eric, and Ron Bradford and his wife Mindi and 6 grandchildren and 1 great granddaughter. They have brought much joy to my life.

The Charloe Store is a place I visit - the girls there are wonderful friends, Crystal, Angel, Kim, Megan. They make my day complete!

The Cooper Community Library is an asset to the village of Oakwood. Sue and Pam work hard to try to meet all of our needs.

Larry and I have retired. He worked 42 years at Cooper Farms, 27 years as manager, then the last 15 in maintenance. I retired after 42 years of doing hair.

Last but not least I have to be thankful for "Our Quarterly Lunch Crew" Michelle Hemker, Robin Adkins, Becky Jo Thomas and Carissa Cohan Eitniear. We have all worked together in the past and have stayed good friends. I have to admit it is rare we all like the place we are going to – but that is women for you.

The 1950 Bridge across the Auglaize River

The "new" bridge was opened with great pageantry and fanfare on October 28, 1950. Approximately three thousand people attended the dedication of the bridge on Route 113 (now 613). A parade was held to mark the event and appearing in the parade were ten high school bands, 13 beauty queens from northwestern Ohio, many individuals in costume, and several floats. The Continental High School band won first place in the band contest and the Paulding High School band took second place. Lois Freed of Melrose won the contest for best costume out of a field of about 200 entries. The prize for best float went to the one from the Huff and Puff Restaurant. Anne Balcz, of Ney, was judged best baton twirler and Patty Peters of Oakwood, was crowned "Corn Festival" queen.

Following the dedication, a turkey dinner was held in the school gymnasium, followed by square and round dancing and a Halloween celebration. Tickets for the dinner were sold at a cost of $1.50

The new bridge was a 309-foot steel truss structure, and was the first bridge of this type built in northwest Ohio. It cost $333,524.84 and was constructed by the Ruckmann-Hansen Company of Fort Wayne, Indiana. It consisted of three spans which were 28 feet wide. The overhead framework had a clearance of fourteen feet. A sidewalk was built along the north side of the bridge.

After the 1913 flood, the car bridge is lying in the river.

Construction was started in September, 1949 and it replaced a 50 year old steel bridge that had been washed into the river during the 1913 flood. After the flood, the bridge had been lifted back onto its foundations and returned to service. Before construction started, the old bridge was moved to the north of its original location and set on temporary pilings so that traffic across the river could be maintained. In the spring of 1950, high water in the river caused the temporary closing of the "old" bridge because there was concern about the pressure of the river's flow against the temporary pilings.

Jeanne Bennett Calvert

The Prairie Creek Bridge

Prairie Creek is the small stream on the north end of Oakwood. The first bridge to cross it was built in 1890. It had a plank floor and was built with no grading. In fact the approach to it was downhill. In 1905, the grade was raised and large sand stones were brought from Indiana for the abutments.

When the new bridge was constructed in 1954, these stones were moved to the skating rink parking lot.

In 1915, an iron bridge was built and in 1926, that bridge was "remodeled." It remained in place until 1954 when it was removed and a new bridge constructed.

The 1954 bridge was 33 and a half feet wide, 86 feet long and cost $35,000 to construct.

Bringing in the New Year!

Happy New Year! That's right another new year and another number to get used to. When I was a young boy, my father celebrated the New Year by going out and firing his 12 ga shotgun 5 times at about the stroke of midnight. It was a memorable experience because Dad would wake us up, get us dressed and take us out the back door with him to "bring in the New Year". Of course I did not understand what that meant but it was dark outside and it was fun to watch the fire shoot out of the end of the barrel of the shotgun. My Mom said that she was afraid we would wake the neighbors, but almost as she was saying it we could hear some of the neighbors' guns go off as they too were celebrating the start of a New Year. When my Dad announced to us that it was not 1952 but the New Year 1953 had begun, I really did not know what he was talking about at the ripe age of 6. Later in school the teacher explained it and I began to understand that this change was important and that it happened every year. One year my sister was too tired to get up so she watched out her upstairs bedroom window as dad shot the gun. Later she told me that the flames out of the barrel came almost as high as the middle of her window and scared her to death. When I grew older (I was 12) and had received a shotgun (it was a 20 ga bolt action) of my own for Christmas, Dad let me take my gun out and help him "bring in the New Year". At the stroke of midnight he fired his 12 ga and I fired my 20ga as soon as he fired his. It was almost like one long blast with the end being somewhat weaker than the beginning. Then we waited for the neighbors to fire their guns and Dad and I fired shot number two. Again we waited and fired shot number three, that was it for me because I only had three shots, but Dad had two more and within a few minutes 1958 turned into 1959 and it seemed to me like it was not that long ago when we had brought in the year 1958….and now it was gone. Dad would tell us that the old year was now history.

Rev. William Sherry

Writing for the Paulding County Progress

John Brown

John Brown was sometimes the contracted janitor at the Oakwood Post Office. John was a sickly young man and when I met him he was in his late 30's and still had health issues. That didn't stop us from playing practical jokes on one another at the office. We each had our Achilles heel. John was deathly afraid of snakes, Dee Back Smith was afraid of mice and I couldn't stand the smell of perfume. When John made me mad, which he did a lot, I would pull out the rubber snake I kept in my stamp drawer. Funny thing for having health issues John could run pretty fast when he saw a snake, even a fake one.

Once we had a mutual friend Diane Bair sent him a picture of a snake in a box. That was a good day, well for Dee and I it was. John, not so much, he opened the box and when he saw the picture the box flew and John went home mad. I guess I did his cleaning that day so I paid for the joke.

John and I had a fake mouse that seemed to find its way into Dee's desk or drawer or stack of reports. We would wait patiently for Dee to find the mouse and the screaming would begin. I never knew mice could fly. John and I would be crying with laughter every time.

I didn't get left out of the deal. Once after I had scared John with the snake he decided to get even with me. I made the big mistake of walking away from my money drawer and John used Dee's perfume and sprayed the coins. Every time I opened the drawer to get out stamps and give change I would have a sneezing fit. I ended up having to wash each and every coin and the drawer and get new bills from the bank.

The best joke was when I convinced John if you sat on a tombstone at midnight on a certain day you could talk to that person and they could answer you. Well, I must say I was pretty persuasive. The story I heard was John convinced someone to go with him to a cemetery at midnight. Unfortunately the cemetery had been having trouble with vandals and they got caught in the cemetery. John never did tell me about having to go to court but his sister did!

We had a great time working at the Post Office and the practical jokes made our day go a little faster. Sometimes it made John's day go so fast that it didn't even begin. Like the time I made a ghost and I attached it to a light in the furnace room where John hung his coat. When I heard his car I ran to the back and spun the ghost on a rubbery string around the light. I ran back and was putting mail in the boxes when John walked in the back door. When John opened the furnace room door all he could see was a white ghost flying around the room. The door slammed and John went home for the day. Once again, I had to clean but it was worth it.

John got even with me once without really trying. He stopped and picked a bouquet of wild flowers to bring in for Dee and I. After about ten minutes I was sneezing and my eyes were red. That was when I found out that although ragweed is very pretty I am very allergic to it. The Post Office would get an uninvited guest from time to time. There was a crack somewhere in the roof and bats could find their way in. Since Dee and John were both afraid of bats it was my job to chase the bats out with a broom. Once when John was walking across the room a bat dived past him. John was just like an old cartoon. He jumped in the air and his legs were going fast but he wasn't moving. After I finished laughing I got the broom and chased the bat out the back door.

We had fun at the Post Office and we still got the job done. Of course, sometimes I got to do his job and sometimes I sneezed my way through my job. No matter who was at the losing end of the joke, we still laughed and were friends until the day he died.

By Shelly Roughton

Anita Burt: "accordin' to my tell"

This title was from a passage in the first edition of "The Hoosier Schoolmaster" by Edward Eggleston. It represents a colloquialism frequently used by early storytellers to indicate that the narrative they were about to tell was as they knew it personally, and not necessarily the way you might tell it.

A favorite family history passed on to this location where I've been calling 'home' for many years. Back in the summer of 1835 Samuel Reid arrived after 3 days on horseback from the Chillicothe area. He began looking for a place to build a grist/lumber mill. All this Black Swamp area was full of rivers, streams with wonderful timber all over. People settling, clearing farmland and building homes and communities. There were a number of mills in the area. Reid found this site upstream from what we know as Fort Brown. Permission was given that he could build a retaining dam of six feet high. Thus the water wheel was laid on its side. While there are no remnants of the wheel or grindstones, etc., the cut-in bank is still visible when the water is lowered in the spring and fall at the Power Dam. You can still see where the dam crossed the bottom of the river and some of the timber-work still remains due to water preservation.

Reid eventually sold it to his son-in-law, Alex Brown. It thrived for some years. Flour and timber came from the mill. A stick the right size was brought in to build coffins, Mrs. Brown lined them. A lane could be seen for years along the river's edge from Gate's Run (Co Rd 177) to the mill and it turned to the west around the mill and house towards the Village of Fort Brown. This was plotted with streets, lots and a post office.

Some years back I found an article about the Leffel turbine, a horizontal iron wheel completely submerged. But though interesting, I don't think there was one used here. When moving earth around in the 1960's we discovered and filled a rock lined dug well. As close to the water as it was it was completely dry.

Other things I remember: Labor Day – setting up the Art Fair fencings around the front of the Oakwood School; the exhibitors also set up exhibits and gave demonstrations; The Boy Scouts and their chicken BBQ pit; the many high school bands who were part of the big parade; Honored Citizen: Mr. John Richardson and his horse and mail buggy.

I also remember steam locomotives, trains that stopped to pick up passengers and putting the mail up to be caught by a hook.

Speaking of trains: Monday was washday. Washboards, wringers, and those clotheslines that were used in the summer. How about getting the wet sheets out and the train engineer blows the whistle for the crossing. Soot everywhere! Including on the wet sheets! A few warm words were called wishing him a safe trip. The lady of the house often made her own wash soap.

Thinking back to school things: Mr. Dunlap's wife, Joan, was very talented in many, many areas. One day their home aquarium's side just blew out! Fish were flopping all over the floor. She quickly gathered them up in a pan and took them over to the high school science room. In the hall several students asked her what she was doing. "I'm taking my fish for a walk." She had a large part in making the Bobcat head for the cheering section. Was Glen Anspach the first student to wear it?

Weather information at your fingertips: Pour coffee into your cup. If there are bubbles in the center, it will be clear. If the bubbles are around the side, it will storm. If the bubbles form at random, there will be a change in the weather.

The graduating class of 1939 was very special to its members. This was just before the Second World War was declared or really thought about too much. The class was full of fun and fellowship. Members of the class had goals of college, work or marriage and were enjoying the freedom of being out of school. Then things really changed for everyone.

Back in the late sixties, we had just moved into a new house when overhead I heard the loud roar of an airplane flying very low. I ran out on the deck; Clyde was out of the studio and in the yard. A fighter jet in black and orange turned and flew in a large circle back around Oakwood and down over our house. It tipped a wing and flew off into the "sunset". Yes, it was classmate Col. Ted Timbers. I've been told that in retirement he was one of several pilots still enjoying the 'air'. He flew for Wayne Newton among others.

Members of the class of '39 enjoyed the Oakwood Homecoming. We worked on several plays for entertainment. Violet Harmon was one who enjoyed doing that. She and Bertie Taylor also worked with the Melrose Institute over the years. What laughter rang out as we worked together. Once live chickens flew out over the crowd. Hazen Bosworth wore a real kilt. Tennison Guyer who later became a U.S. Congressman spoke four times at the Melrose Institute.

Friends now gone but always remembered include Delbert and Zelpha Shisler. They and their mink farm on the Auglaize River over into Putnam County made a great place to go for some relaxation. We would talk of Audubon, Indian mounds, and raising mink. We'd watch hornet nest busy workers and raccoons from the kitchen window. Then go outside for a walk through their fields and along the river. They showed us where they had found a tiny silver coin….could it have been lost by one of Anthony Wayne's men? Delbert always claimed that Wayne's troops had gone through this area as they traveled north along the river. About a mile north of Delbert's was a beautiful Girl Scout day camp. It was heavily used by the Oakwood scouts.

The first people I met when coming to Oakwood were Mick Huff (owner of the Huff 'n Puff restaurant) and Mr. and Mrs. Walter May. Mick was a close friend of Clyde's and they used to watch boxing on Mick's little TV.

Chet Thrasher designed a 'Chester Sight' along with raising turkeys and art. He sponsored a ball team and Mick was the manager. The manager's grey shirt had a beautiful pheasant scene embroidered on the back. Years later, he had the shirt framed so it could be enjoyed by all.

Burt and Sherry's Market

In the 1960's the grocery store in Melrose was run by two octogenarians who wanted something to do in retirement and who also wanted to benefit the community by maintaining a local store.

The low red building was first built on the west side of the street by Bob Patterson who used it for a saloon. Later his wife started a grocery store in the building. She later sold the business to Howard Keck, who sold it to Hal Stump. The next owners were Jess and Retha Sherry, who after a few years sold it to Eddie Fry. He in turn sold it to Henry Coil. When Mr. Coil was ready to sell, Jess Sherry and Alexander (Alex) Burt decided to go back into the world of business. They offered a nice selection of food at reasonable prices. One of the highlights of their business was the large selection of candy which brought a gleam to the eyes of local children. During the winter the store was heated with a large stove.

Both Alex Burt and Jess Sherry lived most of their lives in and around Melrose. Alex was a descendent of the Brown family, who were the first to run a water propelled mill at Fort Brown. What a coincidence that a man by the name of Alex Brown should set up a mill at the location of the fort by the same name. Alex's grandfather, Mark Brown came to Paulding County from Morrow County in the 1860's. He cleared forty acres three miles north of Oakwood and built a log cabin. His son, Theodore, married Eliza Brown, a daughter of the Alex Brown who had set up the mill at Fort Brown. Theodore, Alex Burt's father, at one time ran a packet on the canal and hauled both goods and passengers from Delphos and Defiance and back. Alex and his brothers would follow or ride the packet boats from town to town and help tend the locks. Alex and his wife, Ferrel (Straley) were the parents of Richard, Theodore, Jr., Phyllis Mohr and Joyce Wyatt.

When the Burt's first came to Melrose, it was a promising village. There were lumber factories, sawmills, a tile mill, a hoop factory, and many residences. There also was a hotel, four saloons and a millinery shop managed by Alex's sister, Arminta Burt.

There was a swing bridge where the Nickel Plate Railroad crossed the canal. One time the canal bridge was up and a train ran off the tracks into the canal. Needless to say, that caused a lot of excitement.

Jess Sherry was the son of James and Minnie (Plumb) Sherry. He was born in Allen County, Ohio where his father was a school teacher. Jess's grandfather Albert served in the Civil War. Jess taught school for several years and then became a farmer. He ran a hay-baler for several years and was gone for days at a time as he baled hay over much of northwest Ohio. He also served on the Melrose Board of Education and for a while, ran the Oakwood newspaper.

Based on an article in the Crescent News 1962

Business places in Oakwood

In 1905, there were these businesses and business people:

Marcy and Whitney Elevator; E. Wiseley Dry Goods; D. E. Bobenmyer General Store; Wm. Kirkendall & Son Hardware; M. E. Bidlack Hardware; Counsellor's Restaurant; Bidlack and Kretzinger (George B.) and George K.) barbers; B. L. Caskey furniture and Undertaker; Cudhea's Drug Store; H. S. Robison Lumber and Building Supplies; J. L. Cox Meat Market and Stock Buyer; Bertha Bidlack, Millinery; R. M.

Weible's General Store; L. D. Kohler Photo Studio; Oakwood Bank with C. H. Allen as president, E. Wiseley vice president and A. E. Reid, cashier; Drs. A. C. and E. E. Sherrard and Dennis Cudhea; Oakwood News, Clarence L. Heller, editor and publisher; John J. Alspach, blacksmith; Postmaster Dennis Cudhea; Superintendent of Oakwood School L. F. Chalfant; Nickel Plate R. R. agent Charles H. Russell and Charles A. Jenkins at the Nickel Plate pumping station.

W.V. Kretzinger

Writing in the Oakwood News, May 1955

Later businesses included:

Ackerman's Piano Sales; a livery stable; Dean Lighthill Photography; Sam Shisler's pony barn; C. F. Moorman Hi Speed gas station; John M. Harmon Rexall Store; "Shorty" O'Bryant's Restaurant; Hosler's General Store; Burr Lighthill, dealer in hay, straw and coal; Kohn's Hardware; J. W. Brown, The Green Tea Room; Oakwood Maid Pastry Shop; Bob's Clean Market; Robenolts's Meat Market; Oakwood Oil Company; The Johnson Oil Company; L. A. Crawford's station; Holmes Poultry Plant; Grimm's Blacksmith shop; "Charley" Burt's harness shop; Paul Ice Chevrolet Sales; H. C. Frederick, agent of Ray N. Whitney – the Union Central Life Insurance Company; E. J. Stover's pool room; Joseph Oglesbee, Cream station later Harness and Shoe Repair; Oakwood General Insurance Agency – B. G. Shepard; Hixon Peterson Lumber Company; Fruchey's general store; Bates Hardware; Virgil Miller's Hatchery; Bray's Red and White Store; Winchester's Grocery; Kohart's Salvage Yard; Burnett's Radio Repair; Glen Stores Chevrolet Sales; Earl Williams' Hardware; The Oakwood News – Ward Matson; "Deak" Williams' card room; Ira Mohr's Cream Station; Jenkins Barber Shop; Bidlack Barber Shop; Kohart Barber Shop; Ray Hornish Hardware; Ray Hornish John Deere dealer; Dick Hornish Hardware; Bell's Restaurant; Harris Ford Sales; Stores and Sherman Lumber Yard; Arlo Brand's grocery store; Dunlap's grocery store; Schutz Coal Yard; Hill's feed mill;

Keck's new and used furniture store; A. F. Burson, M. D.; Rickner's garage; Frank Shisler's Livestock Sales; Les Shisler's auto sales, R. C. Christy, insurance; Timbers coal yard.

From a list compiled by "Bill" Harmon, former mayor of Oakwood

Bill Harmon's service station.

It was located between the town hall and what is now Phil's Diner.

First Street in 1938

Bennewell Logan Caskey

Owner of Logan Caskey and Son Funeral Home located in a building on the west side of First Street in downtown Oakwood. The building burned in 1946 and is now the home of the State Bank. Logan Caskey was born October 2, 1870. He died on April 4, 1943.

B. L. Caskey's and Kohn and Goodwin Hardware

"Loge" Caskey as he was called, lived just north of the old Oakwood School, across the street from my great uncle and great aunt Wash and Jenny German – the home now occupied by Mark and Jeanette Figert. The Caskey home was removed with the building of the new Oakwood Elementary School.

Bennewell Logan Caskey, a tall man with a generous paunch, was married to Nan Caskey and had a son, Harry, and a daughter Blanche Caskey Moorman that many of us knew.

Harry Caskey, a short and stout man, worked in the funeral home with his father and passed away a year prior to his father's death. Sources say that his passing caused a great deal of mental grief for his family, especially his father Logan who never really adjusted to the loss of his son.

Daughter Blanche Caskey Moorman graduated from Oakwood High School in 1911 and attended both the Defiance College and Ohio Northern University. She was an elementary school teacher in various Paulding County Schools including Oakwood and was employed by the Paulding County Social Services as a case worker.

Della Stanton and Blanche Caskey

After assuming ownership of the German property, across the street from the Caskey residence, I chose to remove the old barn on the rear of the property. Being sort of picker I chose to look through the barn for any hidden treasures. As luck would have it, I found none. I did find this sign of "B. L. Caskey and Son Funeral Home" that was a part of their hearse and elected to keep it as a piece of Oakwood History.

I would like to say thanks to Bandy Teegarden, Spike Sherman, Verda Leatherman and Helen Maddock for their firsthand knowledge of Bennewell Logan Caskey.

Jim Shisler

Speaking at a cemetery Walk September 2013

Ross Rau was a long time employee of the Caskey and Son Funeral Home. He worked there for twenty-three years.

When he first went into business, Mr. Caskey had a furniture store as well as an undertaking establishment. He later discontinued his line of furniture.

At the time Caskey's were in business, many people had viewing of the deceased in their own home. Sometimes though, if the family did not want those arrangements, the viewing would be held at the Caskey home beside the school. If the deceased person was someone prominent in the community, the school pupils were taken to the Caskey home and allowed to pay their respects.

Mr. Caskey was a diabetic and his death was very sudden following surgery at Lutheran Hospital in Fort Wayne, Indiana

Harry and Logan Caskey with their horse drawn hearse

The Undertakers

Logan Caskey and his son, Harry, had an undertaking business. Everyone, probably, trusted Log and Harry with their bodies – the bodies of their loved ones. Log was a big man physically and Harry was small in stature. I believe Log got the bodies and Harry finished them. Harry and Log were very affable people. They and theirs fit very well in the community.

My husband as a young fellow, was among a group of teenagers who often "passed" time in Oakwood and on some occasions Log would call to the boys, "come on, we have a body to get." And some would always volunteer to go with him, my husband on occasion being one of them. Probably nothing like that would happen today.

Another instance that probably would not happen today is the following: As a little girl, my sister and I were walking uptown when we passed the area where we could see the back room of the "undertaking" parlor. Since it was summer, the door was open (no general air-conditioning then) to what was the "working" part of the building. We were drawn to walk across to see what was taking place in there. In the room were tall poles and fixtures (such as those used for administrating IV's) and metal looking tables such as one might see in operating rooms. There had been a tragedy in our area. A man had "lost it" and shot his wife and daughter, killing them. On those tables and by those poles were the bodies of a small girl and a young woman. There were white sheets over the bodies, but not the faces. Body fluids were being drained from them. I remember how beautiful the faces were (even though one could see holes in their heads) Such a sad sight – especially for little girls!

Submitted by Kathryn Sharp Deatrick

Wondering

As with most every business, there are "happenings." On the main street of Oakwood were the furniture store and the areas for viewing caskets (one's future home). Bill Schilt was a boy who grew up in our community and did odd jobs and took employment where he could. What his job was in the furniture store I do not know – probably helped Log and Harry with the furniture, caskets, and so on…

In those days, the funeral "furniture" was in a furniture store. One selected the casket and the "departed one" was placed in that casket and taken back to the home for viewing. A wreath was hung on the door of that home, denoting the place as a way of informing others that the loved one was inside and respect for the place should be shown. People even used to drive "respectfully" past the house with the wreath on it and salesmen did not knock on the door.

One day, while Bill was working in the store doing odd jobs, he wondered (so the story goes) what it would be like to lie in the casket. So – he did! I don't remember who caught him in it (or rescued him) and I've always wondered if the lid was up or if it was down!

Submitted by Kathryn Sharp Deatrick

Robert Christy

Robert Christy and his wife, Essie, lived on the corner of Auglaize Street where it turns to the east. Bob operated his own business, Christy Insurance which was housed in a small building between the "old" post office and the town hall. The building has since been torn down. Bob and Essie were the parents of one son, Robert, Jr. He became the superintendent of Delphos Public Schools. At one time, Bob owned the farm where my husband and I now live.

The thing that I most remember about Bob was that he led the singing at the Oakwood Methodist Church. After Sunday school, we would have closing exercises. They would ask if anyone had had a birthday in the

Bob and Essie Christy on their 50th anniversary

past week. The "birthday" person would stand up and then Bob would say, "Let's all stand in honor of this birthday." As a child, I always wanted to be sure to be there when it was my birthday. Then Bob would lead us in the closing hymn. He always chose one of the old standards. The one that we sang the most frequently must have been his favorite. I never hear these words, nor sing this song without remembering Bob Christy: "Just every day, God shows the way, How we can help someone, Just every day."

Jeanne Bennett Calvert

Civil Defense

In the midst of the "cold war", Civil Defense organizations were formed not only in all major cities but also in the rural areas of America. In 1955, Everett Wann, Paulding County Civil Defense Director, announced the beginning of a campaign to organize five ground observation corps posts in Paulding County. These plans were made at the direct request of the Air Force Air Defense Command who thought that such posts were needed at Oakwood, Payne, Haviland, Antwerp and Paulding.

Archie "Mick" Huff volunteered to be the supervisor of the Oakwood post.

Do you remember the Coal Yard?

It was located on the east side of N. Sixth Street, along the railroad tracks. There was a 6 foot wooden fence all around it where they kept the different kinds of coal. They also had a large open cistern on the north side of the building that was used to keep the coal dust down – it also had large goldfish in it that we got to feed.

There were different kinds or grades of coal that you could pick from. During the spring/summer months there was a "pickle grader" inside the building. The farmers would bring trucks or trailer loads of pickles for grading and sizing.

This business was owned by my grandparents, Ed and Ida Timbers in the early 1950's. They purchased it from Midge and Oscar Schilt.

Charlene Thomas Stucky

The Coal Yard

The first part of the lumber shed was built by Henry Robison in 1902. In 1903, Claude Morris bought it and built the office and driveway. The logs were hauled to the Henry Varner Saw Mill by Burr Lighthill and then the lumber was hauled to Oakwood to build an addition on the lumber shed.

Claude Morris put up a stockyard back east of the office. Here he bought stock and loaded it on the railroad cars. Shortly after this Claude Morris sold out to Whitney who used the building for an elevator and storing hay.

Later this building was used as a weigh station for the sugar beet company. As a boy I used to go up to see them shovel beets into railroad cars. There used to be ten or twelve teams of horses waiting to unload. Everyone took pride in their team of horses but Carl and Nile Weible each had a team of mules of which they were exceptionally proud. Carl's team of mules was snow white and Nile's were sorrel.

Whitney owned this building until 1920 when it was bought by Burr Lighthill and used for storing and shipping hay. He usually shipped 40 car loads a year. I used to watch them load hay in the box cars. They had to fit them in like a quilt in order to get enough tons in a car.

Later Burr started in the coal business which he built up to 50 car loads a year.

Rodney Shinaberry shoveled off the cars of coal and for a number of years Vern Lighthill was the office man, both working for Burr.

Burr ran the coal yard until 1943 at which time he retired and sold the business to Oscar and Midge Schultz. Since his retirement, Burr has spent a lot of time fishing and traveling,

After Oscar's death, his wife ran the coal yard for a couple of years, and then sold it to Ed Timbers. Ed ran the coal yard until his death when his wife took over. George Stahl of Melrose managed the business for her.

Later he ran a junk yard in the building for a short time before Ina Timbers sold the building and ground to the Oakwood Development Corp. It was then used as a tomato weigh station and I can still see John Rau loading semi-trucks with tons of tomatoes.

Gerald Shisler then rented it and used it as a storage place for his boat business.

The past few years, the building has stood empty. Here it had a hard life. Someone broke all the windows and doors out of the building.

The building was auctioned off by Charles Cunningham who sold it without charge. The building was bought by Harley, Jack and Nolan Shisler with an agreement to tear it down. Laurel Carnahan bought the scales for $50. Porter and Switzer of Melrose bought the loader and motor for $220. Thus retires the coal yard and lots of hard work.

Harley Shisler

Writing in the Oakwood News

Dial Telephones

In the spring of 1955, the local members of the Oakwood Telephone Company Board were divided on the matter of whether or not the company should convert to a dial system. The state Public Utilities Commission had come out with new standards that were to become effective in 1956 and the local board had to decide whether they should spend money to come up to the minimum standards or to borrow money from the REA and convert the system to dial. Included in the new standards were the requirements that long distance service must be available 24 hours a day and there could be no more than 10 subscribers on a "party" line. In 1955, there was one line in the Oakwood system with 17 subscribers and others had 14 and 12 subscribers. At that time, the switchboard closed at 10:30 PM. But the chief operator, Mrs. Katie McClure, lived in the same building where the telephone company was located and was available for emergency calls in the night.

At that time, rates were $2.25 for a party line and $3.00 for a private line. Business rates were $3.00 for a party line and $4.00 for a private line. Only a limited number of private lines were available.

In 1955, operators were handling approximately 50 long distance calls a day with the record being 89. These calls had to be handled through Paulding and in some cases that proved to be a bottle neck. It was estimated that it would cost $180,000 to make the conversion to dial and that this would raise the monthly bill by $2.00.

Opponents to the conversion felt that many members would have their phones removed if the rates were raised and there was also concern that older subscribers would have trouble learning to use the new dial system.

Jeanne Bennett Calvert

Julius and Marie Dobbelaere

Julius and Marie Dobbelaere came to the United States on their honeymoon. They were from southern Belgium and both of their families had suffered during the First World War.

Marie and most of her family had fled to France when their homeland was overrun by the German army. At the time, Marie was on summer vacation from boarding school when suddenly their village was overrun with German soldiers. They collected a few belongings and left for France. They stayed there for four years and when they returned found only rubble where their home had been. Still they rejoiced because their family had survived….not the case for half of the people in their small community who did not survive.

Julius had joined the Army and he had also survived. But like Marie, his family had lost their home and livestock. His family did own land and he could have remained and became a father like his father. However, farming was dangerous as there were still unexploded bombs buried in the fields. After four years as a soldier, he was eager to see something of the world. At first he thought about moving to France and farming there. But like Belgium, there was so much damage in France this did not seem like an improvement. Julius had a cousin living in Michigan and he decided that might be the answer.

Marie did not want to leave her family and home but she and Julius were in love and wanted to get married. They married on April 1, 1920 and soon after left for the United States. Marie said she cried and cried as they left. Julius told her parents that they would return as soon as they could save enough money. It took almost all of their money to pay for their passage to the United States. It was over five years before they were able to return to Belgium for a visit.

Arriving at Ellis Island was a frightening experience for Marie. She did not speak English at that time and found the whole process very confusing and scary. They first went to Monroe, Michigan, where Julius's cousin lived. He suggested that there were better ways to get ahead in the world than by being a farmer. But Julius wanted to farm.

At first Julius worked in a sugar beet factory and farmed part time. The young couple moved to Wood County, Ohio, where Julius farmed for an elderly man. They hoped to buy that farm but the owner died and their plans fell through. Then they saw an advertisement in the Toledo newspaper for farm land for sale in Paulding County. They came to

Paulding County and bought a small farm. Later they were able to buy a larger farm. By now they had 7 children: 6 boys and a girl.

Then in 1947, tragedy struck: Julius died. Marie's sister in Belgium urged her to return with her five school aged children. But the older children did not want to leave the United States and they prevailed on their mother to remain.

Based on an article in the Farmland News in 1987

The Oakwood Elevator

The old wooden elevator was torn down during the summer of 1956 forcing the suspension of grinding and mixing services during the construction period. The old elevator had been built by J. W. Whitney. Construction on the "new" elevator began on August 1, 1956 and by November 3, 1956, the job was finished. The cost of the construction was approximately $125,000.

The Whitney Elevator

The bins of the new elevator were 95 feet tall and had a total storage capacity of 60,000 bushels. The round metal bins which were constructed in 1950, had a capacity of 50,000 bushels of grain.

The new corn sheller that was installed was capable of shelling 1,200 bushels of corn per hour. Odey Mumy was the manager of the facility at that time.

Charles Estle

Charles Richard Estle was born on June 19, 1912. He was a child that loved school, and never hated to get up to go to school. His father was a doctor, and Charles would go with his father on house calls. He even had an opportunity to witness babies being born. Charles' father delivered over ninety babies as a doctor. Charles remembers going on visits with his father in the horse and buggy. He also remembers what an exciting moment it was when his family got their first car.

After high school, Charles worked as a lab technician for Firestone Tire and Rubber. He then went to Ohio University and received a Bachelor's Degree in education.

Mr. Estle and Virginia Pessefall

Charles was a combat engineer in the army. He was in the 9th division and served in the European theater four days after D Day. His division went to Utah Beach in Europe. He married Mildred "Lucille" in 1934 and they lived in Athens while he worked on his master's degree in School Administration at Ohio University.

Charles was the Superintendent for the Oakwood schools from 1945 – 1955. He served as a principal in the Chilicothe schools from 1955 – 1975. He continued to work in the Chilicothe school system in the area of curriculum, retiring in 1980.

At that time, he and Lucille returned to Oakwood to be near their only son, Marvin, and his family. Charles and Lucille had six grandchildren and Charles always supported them in their activities, going to many sporting events. He continued that practice for his great-grandchildren. He was an avid OSU football fan and attended many home games in Columbus.

He once related this funny story: He and Lucille were driving in the car and stopped in McArthur, Ohio where they got out of the car at a filling station. When it was time to get back in the car, there was a female sitting in the passenger side of the car. He just assumed it was his wife. He drove down the road a ways and then looked over at the person he thought was his wife. To his astonishment, it was another woman. Apparently she had gotten in the wrong car. He returned to the place where he had previously stopped and there was his wife talking to the other lady's husband. They had a good chuckle over that.

Apache Specht Etter Remembers:

In the early 40's my grandmother Amelia Specht lived in a small house across the lane from our farm house. She would make just plain Jello. My mother always put fruit in her Jello. I would go over to her house and eat her Jello. Grandmother made a good chop suey but we never got her recipe.

We took Grandma Amelia to Newark, N. J. to visit her sister-in-law Sophia. I wanted to see the ocean. Never saw it, just played in the sand. When I was 5 Grandma and I got on the train at Oakwood and went to Englewood station in Chicago to visit family. The "L" went behind their apartment. The noise kept me awake all night. I got homesick.

In the 50's, Oakwood had a free show in the park every Saturday night after the sun went down. For a short time, they had shows on Wednesday nights. Dad would go to Lester Shisler's car dealership to visit. Mon would visit her folks who lived across the street from the school. One night Mom and I went to the Huff & Puff restaurant for a hot fudge Sunday. We went to our car to wait for Dad. When he came he to us to the Huff & Puff for a hot fudge Sunday! The second Sunday wasn't as good as the first. We never told Dad.

George Specht standing by flood waters north side of Oakwood

June 1950, the Auglaize River is out of its banks. George Specht is standing by Neese Run on Route 66, north of Oakwood. This is the only time that I saw water over the road at this location.

June 1950 Looking north from the viaduct

The Carnahan cousins had fun playing at Grandpa Carnahan's farm. The farm was north of Oakwood. We would take blankets out in the front yard and when a car would drive by we would get under the blankets. We thought they couldn't see us!

The Carnahan cousins left to right: Dale Carnahan drives truck; Mary Carnahan Clay lives in Florida; Donna Jean Carnahan Gerschutz is deceased; Apache Specht Etter lives on Rd 122; Bruce Carnahan; Richard Carnahan lives on Rd 179.

Dad left me twice in Oakwood. He would go to bed and ask Mom if I was home. The first time Donna and Todd brought me home. The second time I went to Grandmother Carnahan's house and went to bed. Dad had a hard time finding me.

Labor Day Weekend was always busy. Grandpa Marion and Grandma Elise had their family bring food. We would go to the school grounds and when we got hungry we would go to their house. The parade was the highlight of Monday.

This was Louise Hosler's Float. Those on the float are Donna Jean Carnahan Gerschutz, Elise Carnahan, Apache Specht Etter, Pat Bradford Spitnale. Louise had her beauty shop in the former location of Dr. Burson's office. It is now the south part of the Landing Strip. Later her shop was located on Rd. 191 near her home.

Our family has walked the Mackinac Bridge (five miles) on Labor Day 1990 to 2001. Then in 2008 our family walked for our 50th wedding anniversary. One year we took Mary Evelyn Etter across in a wheelchair. We have a lot of good memories.

Ed took his wife and 3 kids (Jill 5, Kelly 3, and Len 2) fishing back of house on the Auglaize River. Ed was very busy helping everyone to keep their lines in the water. Someone got a small turtle. The kids got their picture taken with the turtle.

Len Etter with the turtle

Ed Etter with his 25" pike

Ed was a good teacher for two of his children who like to fish. Every July we spend two weeks on Sugar Island. We fish the St. Mary's River that runs from Lake Superior to Lake Huron. We have caught some large 33" and 39 ½" northern pike and small 10" pike.

In January, Hocking Hills has a winter hike. Sometimes it is cold enough to freeze the water falls; other years it is warm enough the water is still running. Donna, Ed and I walked for five years. One year it was below zero and our cameras would freeze up. We would walk 3 miles then have beans and corn bread. The next year we took some packets of ketchup.

Ed, Apache Etter and Donna Roughton in the Hocking Hills

One fall, Ed, Donna and I found a tree back by the Auglaize River with lots of hickory nuts on the ground. We wondered why the squirrels didn't eat them. We picked up a large burlap bag of nuts. On the way home, we had to cross a small creek. We dropped the bag and lost half of the nuts. So for the second time, we picked up nuts. When we got home we cracked some. They were PIG nuts and no one will eat them. We had a big bag of nothing!

The Everwilling Home Demonstration Club

The Everwilling Home Demonstration Club was organized October 21, 1947, by Mary Herman, Paulding County Home Demonstration Agent, in the home of Ethel Specht. She and Helen Thomas had attended some meetings in Paulding as there were several clubs already organized in the west side of the county. Ethel and Helen invited their friends and neighbors to this organizational meeting. Charter members were: Nellie Shisler Rhees, Mary Lois Kohart, Esther Carnahan, Louise Hosler, Ethel Bradford, Elsie Carnahan, Alta Hays, Blanche Horner, Ilo Keck, Ethel Specht, Anna Fuller, Madonna Horner, Cleo Bidlack, Leota Roberts, Helen Thomas, Hilda May, Eunice Bradford, Virginia Cooper and Rosemary Thomas.

During those early years, the meetings were very much "hands on demonstrations". We did textile painting, cleaning and adjusting our sewing machines, made slip covers and repaired the springs in our cushions. We learned how to remove stains, sharpen knives, iron our clothes, mend overalls and darn socks. We also had fun projects such as making aluminum trays, jewelry, phonograph record bowls, etched glass and rugs. We had kitchen planning and everyone was measured for what height their cupboards should be. I really enjoyed having a counter top the right height to roll out pie dough and cookies. We made candy, cookies and bread, learned how to use our broiler and freezer. We even had time management way back in 1965 as well as weight control....some things don't change.

In 1948 the Achievement Meeting was at the Paulding School. Specialists came from Ohio State to share the latest information on clothing and appliances. Walter Barrett was the County Agent and he shared what was happening in Extension. Everyone was to bring used clothing and shoes to be sent overseas. We were the first club organized on this side of the county. By 1952 Friendly Neighbors, Busy Neighbors, Sisters of the Skillet, Know Your Neighbors, West Community Club, Everwilling, Rosehill, Washington Township Neighbors, New and Better Methods and Crane Township were all established clubs. Mary Herman had married and moved to Bryan and Eleanor (George) Brune was the extension agent.

By 1959 there were 16 clubs in the county. The Extension Office was still in the basement of the Paulding Post Office. Pauline Vetter had left as agent and JoAnn Hardesty came.

The Achievement Meetings were the highlight of our club year. Everyone looked forward to wearing their Easter finery, including of course, hat and gloves, renewing friendships from across the county, as well as, hearing interesting speakers, having attendance and name tag contests, seeing displays of projects, relaxers and skits and style shows. I still remember egg dresses, percolator hats and balloon dresses. What fun we had.

March 1952 Front: Esther Carnahan, Ethel Specht, Rosemary Thomas, Ida Kohart, Blanche Horner, Pauline Cooper, Phyllis Lloyd.
Back: Mary Lois Kohart, Hilda May, Eunice Bradford, Annie Fuller, Alice Johnson, Colleen Schick, Cleo Bradford, Madonna Horner, Ethel Bradford, Gladys Kohart. Absent: Nellie Shisler, Helen Thomas, Donna Roughton, Gertrude Keck, Ilo Keck, Emma Helms, Virginia Cooper

JoAnn left as agent and we had Leanne Schwartz, Mary Wiley, Loretta Oakley, Laura King, then Loretta again, Susan Shockey and in 1992 Nancy Stehulak.

We had many interesting Achievement Day Speakers over the years as well as a County Chorus and a Kitchen Band made up of club members. After meeting many years in churches and schools across the County, in 1982 we had our first Achievement Meeting in the new Extension Building at the Fairgrounds.

Our club supported the March of Dimes, Polio Foundation, Cancer Fund, Red Cross, Oakwood Library, the new Paulding Hospital, Christmas Baskets, the EMS and many other projects.

By 1970 times were changing, many women were working outside the home, so we changed to evening meetings. Over the years we had many baby showers, Golden Wedding parties and yes, memorial services for lost members, Christmas parties, County trips and Club trips.

By 1985 there were only 7 clubs in the County, We were planning more and more of our own programs. During the 90's our Achievement Meeting, now called Spring Fling, was being less and less attended and each club now had part of the program rather than having a speaker.

By 1997, when our club celebrated its 50th anniversary, there were only 3 clubs left in the County so the Council voted to disband. The money left in the Council Fund was donated to the renovation of the grandstand at the fairgrounds.

We still meet once a month and usually have 12 – 15 members in attendance. We still have a club trip each year and enjoy having speakers at our meetings as well as crafts, games and other fun activities.

Submitted by Rosemary Thomas

Last active Charter member

April (Spitnale) Ferland Remembers

I have many fond memories of growing up in Oakwood.

Attending school where you knew everyone's name.

Cheering for the Oakwood Bobcats!

Penny pitch & "pitching" the pennies above the door on the ledge at school.

Participating in the Homecoming parade for at least 20 years.

Sitting in the dunking booth for the fire department.

Participating in the waterball tournament also, for the fire department.

Uncle Jim bringing the white fire truck from Grover Hill for the parade.

Eating homemade ice cream.

Election Day dinners.

Bringing my children back to watch the parade & the joy in their faces; especially when candy was thrown from participants.

Growing up in Oakwood: Mom always knew what happened at school before getting home. So it was easier to tell on yourself if you were in "trouble."

I remember going to Lucille Rees' home for religion classes.

Being able to ride my bike all around town without fear.

Being able to play until the street lights come on.

Community feeling like family.

The fire at the elevator.

Many trucks hitting the viaduct.

People waving to you whether you knew them or not.

The Auglaize River flooding.

1974 Tornado.

Playing softball & watching many tournaments at the fields.

Family & friends who will be there for you no matter the need!

Oakwood was a great place to grow up.

Fort Brown

What's in a name? Well. It depends upon what one is looking for. If one is thinking of wealth, Rockefeller comes to mind. Leadership and bravery brings Washington to mind. Lincoln is noted for honesty and love of country. When one thinks of gold, Fort Knox pops up in one's head.

However, a name can be misleading.

Let's take Fort Brown, a small supply fort built where the Little Auglaize River empties into the Auglaize River during the War of 1812. Several supply forts were built as American troops were trying to drive the Indians from Northwest Ohio.

Nothing exciting happened at Fort Brown until a man with vision by the name of Ray Burt decided that the location was ideal for a recreation complex.

During the 1930's Ray had put up a large dance hall. In addition to the dance hall, a baseball field, several cottages, a restaurant, rental boats, a swimming area, a picnic area and a playground became part of the complex that attracted visitors from the tri-state area.

Dancing lasted for a few years, but was limited to the weekends. Ray decided to use the facility for roller skating. That activity made Fort Brown a household name.....

"Grandpa, did you ever skate there?"

Oh, yes, many times and it was fun," I replied.

"Claire, just imagine we're at Fort Brown. We've put on the skates, and we're going around the rink. Be careful and don't fall because you might get a floor burn. Sure good to see Marge Bidlack. Here comes Betty Anne Emerick. She was once May Queen. There goes Anita, she later married Clyde Burt. Don "Slug" Burt was Ray's nephew, as was Clyde. There are several here from Grover Hill, Paulding and Continental."

"Claire, do you see that guy? That's Dick Parrish and he's trying to catch Helen Fitzwater. That tall good looking guy is Gene Wreede."

"Must be an Oakwood skate night, I see Walt Harris, Helen Dunlap, Anna Lee Stover, Tubby and Dave Price, Donna Richardson, Kate and Evalina Sharp, Don Adams and Helen Harris. Sure is nice to see so many friends, but I'm getting tired so it's time to quit."

"Grandpa, are there other things to do at Fort Brown?"

"You bet there were. Every Sunday during the summer there was a ball game that provided entertainment for the crowd that attended."

Fort Brown in the 1930's

Centenary had a team made up mostly of Grimes' and Adams'. Shorty Adams was the manager and did a good job. Later on Harold Williams was their pitcher.

"Earl Williams was the manager of a team composed of local players, mostly from Oakwood. Oakwood and Centenary would take on teams from Ottoville, Grover Hill, Defiance, Paulding and any team that could be scheduled."

"One particular game was special. Al Maddock, who was from Oakwood, was umpiring in the big leagues. He was home on vacation, came out and called the game. We all loved Al. He made that day and the game super special."

"Well, Claire, besides baseball and skating, one could boat, fish, swim, rent a cottage, have a picnic, eat at the restaurant and play the jukebox."

"If one wanted to he/she could boat to Charloe and visit Peppers Store or continue on and view the old steel five span bridge."

"One could also boat up the Little Auglaize which was to say the least, very scenic. One could also boat to the north island and camp for a while. Today the island is no longer present, having been removed by ice and flooding."

Richard Harris

Writing in the Paulding County Progress

Fort Brown Marker

As part of the Ohio State sesquicentennial activities in 1953, a committee was formed to oversee the erection of a permanent marker to mark the location of Fort Brown. Fort Brown was built at the confluence of the Little Auglaize and Auglaize Rivers during the War of 1812.

A site was prepared and the new marker put in place and on August 16, 1953 the marker was dedicated. Governor Frank J. Lausche was the speaker at the dedication. Walter C. May, the grandson of David Carey, the first white child born in Paulding County, had the privilege of unveiling the new monument.

In 2013, the Daughters of 1812 placed a memorial bench at the site.

Charles Estle, Walter May, Harley Shisler on the left
Old Fort Brown Marker

The marker erected in 1953

Fort Brown May Queen

In 1942, Bettyanne Emerick was selected as May Queen at the Fort Brown skating rink.

She is pictured here with her court: Left to right: Carl McClure, Donna Dean Lighthill Eakins, Doris Bauer Mowery, Jo Ann Robnolte Dunlap, Helena Weyrauch Yetter, Nila Ketner Agnes, Evalena Sharp Fitzwater, Betty Badman Noffsinger, Helen Harmon, Helen Rieke Heller Andrews, unknown, Aileen Kirkendall Gordon, Marvel Heffley Kirkendall, Edna McGhan, unknown. In front: Kathryn Euler, crown bearer and Queen Bettyanne Emerick Diamond Taft

The Fowlerton, Texas Connection

In 1910, the town of Fowlerton, Texas was founded by two brothers who described themselves as "colonizers" and advertised land for sale all over the eastern United States. They were attempting to develop 100,000 acres of land that had once belonged to the Dull Ranch. They induced the San Antonio, Uvalde and Gulf Railway to extend its lines into the planned town, built two dams to provide water for irrigation and a new hotel, and laid 200 miles of public roads. They also built a cotton gin, installed an expensive water system, and conducted an aggressive advertising campaign to attract settlers and investors. Locally Leander

1912

Excursion to Texas

1912

Join our crowd and go along to Fowlerton, Texas, where you can buy land for $38 per acre that is worth more than the land here that is selling from $125 to $200 per acre.

If you're from Missouri, give us a chance, and we will show you just what can be done on a 10-acre farm. Now is the time to get in on this while the price is still low, as it will not remain so long.

Land that is cleared and irrigated is worth from $250 to $400 now and it is a known fact that the irrigated land is the highest priced land in the United States, and always will be as a failure is never known. You get a crop every year. Not too wet or not too dry, but just right.

Look on the other side and see what can be produced on one acre of ground in Texas; these statements are not over estimated. Join us on our excursion and see for yourself.

Excursion will leave Continental August 20th or September 3d. For further information, write, phone or call on

L. D. KOHLER
Oakwood, Ohio

David Kohler was their agent. He organized excursions to Texas for area residents. The land was divided into small tracts sold on generous terms. For $25 down and $10 a family could get land for crops AND a nice lot in town. By October 1911, when the SAU&G officially arrived in Fowlerton, the town was prepared with two hotels, three stores, miles of streets, telephones and 1,200 Fowlerites. By 1914, there were over two thousand residents in the town which had its own telephone service. However, a drought struck and many people lost their investment. By 1925, the population had declined to 600 and the community never recovered. Today the population is less than 100 individuals.

Information from John Leffler, "FOWLERTON, TX," *Handbook of Texas Online"*

Hotel Fowlerton at Fowlerton, Texas.
Postcard circa 1913 courtesy William Beauchamp Collection

Marvin C. Fuller: this is your life

In my way of thinking, you are no older than you make yourself act. The key to old age is plenty of hard work and a lot of exercise according to Marvin C. Fuller.

Marvin is eighty-nine years old and is one of the oldest persons in town.

You were born December 4, 1866, three miles north and one half west of Oakwood, Ohio, Paulding County, in the woods owned by your parents, Willis and Nancy Fuller. Willis Fuller was a Civil War veteran. He lost his right arm at Gettysburg. Here in the woods you grew to manhood. Most of your early days were spent cutting timber and working on your father's farm and sawmill.

You and your father cut and sawed the timber that is in the Oakwood Elevator. There was no bridge north of Oakwood over the Prairie Creek by Rickners. It was so wet and muddy that you had to haul the timber by teams three miles east of Oakwood to the railroad and load it on flat cars so it could be hauled to town. When you were a boy you did not have to watch your diet as the axe and crosscut took care of that. You went to school at the Basswood school. The school stood where Ernest Weller now lives. You had a lot of teachers, but your favorite was May Christy. You quit school in the fourth grade to start to work on your father's sawmill that he had on his farm.

On August 7, 1885, at the age of nineteen years, you married Edith Hager. To this family, five boys and five girls were born. They are in order of age: Eathel Fuller, who was never married and who you now live with in Oakwood, was the oldest; Essa, deceased; Imo, deceased; Glenna, who now lives in Arcola, Indiana; Lawrence, deceased; Marshall, deceased; Clyde, deceased; Aden, who now lives at Continental, Ohio; Floyd, deceased; and Lola, deceased. You have had your doors darkened by the death of seven children and two wives.

You moved to town and started a garage, which you ran for twenty years. It was in the building that stood where Merle Dangler's house and little store building now stand (just north of town hall). After you were in the garage and repair shop, you put in the first gasoline that was ever sold in Oakwood. It was Shell gas, which you measured out in five gallon cans and poured out in a funnel. They hauled it over from Continental with a big gray team of horses. I remember the nose bags that they fed the horses out of at noon. You made the first free air compressor that was in Oakwood. Before this you had to pump all tires up with a hand pump. Most of the boys helped you in the repair shop. The old saying is: "It took more matches to keep your pipe lit than any other man in the world." You and all the boys were good repair men. You sold your garage out to Paul Ice and retired. Again, death came to your house, your wife, Edith died in 1932.

In 1934, you went to Ann Arbor, Michigan, and married Bessie Doster, a cousin of your first wife. There you built a new house, gas station and grocery store. You and your wife ran the business for twenty years. Here you gained a lot of new friends, you spent a lot of time fishing out of the lake that was nearby. In the year of 1953, Bessie, your second wife died. Marvin thought he would stay there, sell gas and take life easy. But they had news for you. Bessie had made a will, and everything went to her children. This was a big letdown to you, you worked hard to build a house and store, and at your age it is hard to start life over. You did not let this get you down, only one thing left to do, move back to good old Oakwood with your daughter, Eathel, which you did.

It is no wonder that Rip Van Winkle, after sleeping forty years, did not know a soul when he returned. You were gone twenty years and did not know half of the folks in your home town when you returned. Marvin's hobby is fishing and he spends a lot of time watching TV programs. Your favorite is topnotch wrestling. At the age of eighty-nine, you still walk at least one mile every day. Last week, you caught twenty-two fish in one day. The next day you went fishing behind the city dump which is your old fishing spot, but when you got to the river you had no bait as you had picked up the wrong can.

In closing Marvin said "It has been a short stay as time goes so fast. Oh, why should I complain as I have three good meals a day and television to watch and Eathel to cook for me. My best friend is my pipe. Come back when I am old, and you can write about me again. I have a lot of pleasant memories about Oakwood."

Harley Shisler

Writing for the Oakwood News, April 1955

Henry and Kate Gary

Retired Paulding County farmer and carpenter keeps active at the age of 91. If you want to keep good health and live to a ripe old age, you must keep yourself busy. This, Henry and Kate Gary, have done most of their lives.

Henry, you are the son of F. W. and Katherine Gary. Your father and brothers built a lot of the big barns and houses in our community. There were seven boys and three girls in the family of which you are the only one living. At the age of 17, you helped your father build a barn that Gilbert Schick now owns. You also helped to build the garage that used to be a lumber shed operated by Henry Robinson, and which is now known as the Shisler Garage here in Oakwood. You also built the grist mill that stood back of Ed Timbers home. You received one dollar and twenty five cents per day and your dinner for your work.

You married Kate Forney of Junction, Ohio and to this family two daughters were born. Nellie, the oldest taught school 17 years and at the present time is head librarian at the Defiance County Library. Pauline Ruth was your second blessing; however, she did not stay long. Your door was darkened by her death at the age of 17 months.

You have been a faithful Odd Fellow Lodge member the past 56 years and also a loyal Democrat all of your life. You used to cross the river by fording it and you have crossed all three of the bridges including the new bridge that now stands on 113 in the village of Oakwood.

Henry has lived for 50 years two miles south of Goodwin, and has had good health until the past few weeks. His sickness has kept him in bed quite a bit of the time lately. His hobby was hunting, reading and he likes to have company.

The first church he attended after he was married was a German Reformed Church at Junction. For the past 20 years, Henry has attended the Methodist Church at Melrose. Henry paid $30.00 for his last Model T Ford and sold it for $45.00 after driving it for 10 years.

Kate Forney Gary, 85, has been a faithful wife, mother and housekeeper. She was a school teacher before her marriage. She taught at the Basswood School, located where Virgil Cooper now lives. She received $22.00 a month for teaching. Some of her pupils were: Walter C. May, Perry Bobenmyer, May Brinkman, Frank Shisler, Ed

Timbers and Wilford Kretzinger. Even tho' Mrs. Gary is 85, she is still able to do her own housework.

Harley Shisler

Writing for the Oakwood News

Halloween

Halloween, it's not all that scary today but let me tell you a story that may make you think a little differently!

Sometime in my school experience at Auglaize Brown Local School, we had to read the story about Ichabod Crane and the Headless Horseman of Sleepy Hollow. It was about time for Halloween and it seemed appropriate to do something original. Several of my friends decided to make a headless man from an old shirt and pants that we stuffed with straw. It was quite a work of art with the red poster paint around the headless neck of our creation. With the addition of some old boots it appeared almost real. "Headless" we called him. Well, the question was. "What do we do with this masterpiece?" We could hang him from a bridge for everyone to see and there was a span bridge not too far from where we lived. After much talk, we decided it would be neat to hang our piece of art on the bridge for passing motorists to admire. That is what we would do that night on Halloween. It was a cold, dark Halloween night, we had some trouble getting the rope over the top of the bridge so one of our more agile cohorts crawled up to the top of the bridge with a rope and now "Headless" was not just a statue but we could raise and lower the headless man down in front of an oncoming car or truck and raise it out of the way just in time (before it hit). Oh what fun that would be and certainly more fun that just displaying "Headless" hanging from a bridge. It wasn't long until the first car approached and we dropped "Headless" down in front of an oncoming car and then pulled him back up to the top of the bridge. We had unknowingly concealed our rope in the bridge span and we were well out of sight under the bridge. By the time the motorists stopped, we had "Headless" well out of sight at the top of the bridge. We surprised several passing car loads of the local residents, and then off in the distance we heard the piercing sound of a siren. It was a few miles away but now we were scared. "What if someone had called the Sheriff and he was coming to check out a complaint about our prank?" Down came "Headless" and the rope and off we ran around the corner and across the railroad tracks where we had left our car. Away we went as the flashing lights and siren approached the bridge. We were gone and it was a real relief that we had not been caught. I took "Headless" home and put him in the haymow of the barn. In my opinion, this may be a fictional story coming form an old timer that remembers many Halloween seasons and it may have happened just like I told it.

William Sherry

Writing for the Paulding County Progress

Richard Harris Remembers: The Oakwood I Once Knew

Space but not the memory will limit what I can write about a quaint little village called Oakwood, located in Paulding County, Ohio.

Oakwood had everything a growing up boy needed: Many stores on Main Street, the ice houses, the cattle and horse barns, the railroad, the depot, the Auglaize River, the school and the churches.

The Nickel Plate Railroad ran through the town. L. E. Speakman was the station agent. We would spend much time watching him send messages on the telegraph key. Dot. Dot. Dash - his thumb and finger would go. We watched amazed.

Then it was time to put up the mail sack. He would hang it between two arms by the track. The oncoming passenger train would hook it in, kick off some mail and continue on. My brother and I would get the Sunday paper that way, and deliver it to some of the town people.

Jim McCullough, with his team of horses and wagon, would gather the mail from the stopped trains and make deliveries to the town business places. Watching and riding with him was much fun.

Oakwood had many business places: Fruchey's grocery and dry goods, Ira Mohr's creamery, B. L. Caskey funeral home, Miller's hatchery, Shisler's motor sales, Robinolte's meat market, Hosler's grocery and dry goods and others that will be mentioned later.

During the 20's, the 30's and 40's and several years after WW II, small towns such as Oakwood prospered. Saturday night was the big night. All stores were open, and the streets were filled with shoppers. An ice cream cone, a bottle of pop and a visit with friends made the simple life very enjoyable. Malls in nearby cities were springing up and small towns would begin to suffer.

The Auglaize River flowed through Oakwood, and it was an ideal recreation place. Soon as school was out for the summer, we hurried to the river to go fishing. Oh, what fun to catch bullheads, carp and other varieties of fish. We had a row boat which was ideal for bass fishing. A cane pole and a spinner gave one plenty of excitement. One year the beet plant at Ottawa emptied their refuse into the river killing all the game fish and many other kinds.

We all did a lot of swimming. The railroad had a center support. At the water's edge of the support was a three foot ledge. Make it to this ledge and you were a qualified swimmer. During the winter months the river was perfect for ice skating. The weekends and evenings found many enjoying skating and sledding. On the bank, a large fire added to the scene and the warming of hands.

The hills on my grandpa's farm were just right for sledding. Saturdays found the hills crowded with many fun loving kids.

Ice skating on the Auglaize River

Oakwood had its share of personalities. One man claimed he carried a 320 bowling average. Another claimed he raised three legged chickens. No young guy ever went with him to view that rarity. Another man carried an alarm clock with him. Asked why, he said so he could turn it off if the alarm sounded.

Harry, the bum, came each summer and would jump from the top of the railroad bridge. The crowd would give him the small collection. We also had Ernie, Arty, Joe, Nellie, Erwin, Charlie, Danky and Rose. Each was unique in a special way.

It's true. There was a large manure pile one block west of Main Street. My grandpa, Frank Shisler, had a livestock barn that was usually full of horses and cows. He also had goats. After milking, the cow side was cleaned and the waste piled outside to be hauled away later. The pile grew to be huge.

Sometimes my grandpa would say "Richard, take this horse up to the water tank." The pump was many yards away and the horse was big and full of energy. That was an experience that taught me to avoid the barn at watering time.

Directly across from the horse and cow barn was Matt Robinolte's slaughter house and ice house. Matt was an expert at skinning and butchering cows, pigs, and fur bearing critters. We watched with big eyes. Each winter Matt hired many young guys to help him put up ice. A line of helpers extended from the river to the ice house. As the ice was cut, it would proceed by many hands to the big ice house where it would be covered with sawdust, which kept it from melting. We would later play in the ice house, climbing the covered cakes of ice.

Another large ice house once stood in the area of the present day fire station. A large pond was nearby and was the source of the ice. The ice house and the pond are both gone and houses now occupy the land.

One evening a fire broke out in Hosler's store. Oakwood had an old fire truck. The siren was mounted near the passenger door on the hood and was turned by a crank. The truck carried two large tanks filled with water, soda and acid. Turn the tanks over and the contents became active. Upon arriving at the fire scene, one of the volunteer firemen got so excited; he ran with the hose and disconnected it from the tank. Seeing that they needed help, Defiance was called. They pumped water from the river, but to no avail and the entire building burned to the ground. The band stand and Legion hall occupy the area where the store once stood.

For good eats one could visit the restaurant ran by Harley Shisler, located next to Fred Bray's Red and White Store. One day a large number of Gypsies came to town and caused much excitement as they went from store to store and the eating places.

Towards the railroad was O'Bryant's restaurant. Mae served the best watered down chili in northwest Ohio. If by chance the chili burned a hole in your shoe, a quick fix could be made at Joe Oglebee's shoe repair which was next door.

Oakwood had two bakeries, Coonrods and Browns. Ed Stover moved into Coonrods, selling ice cream, candy, soft drinks, tobacco and beer. His store remained a popular place for many years.

Most young people had a nickname. Adults were often confused during a conversation because of this. If one was referring to Alice Huff, you called her "Punkie" Walter Harris was "Boze", Dean Mohr was "Dizzy". Bud Fuller was "Lardie". Shirley Harris was "Babe". Dale Roughton was "Pablo". Vic Dunlap was "Baron". Glen Weible was "Tim". Gene Bennett was "Moose". Robert Brown was "Beanie". Ned Schultz was "Tom". Don Burt was "Slug" and Bill Huff was "Porky". Lawrence "Sketter" Bidlack will conclude those I wish to mention. Many others, seeing the names listed will think of others, bringing to mind incidents that happened.

School days were filled with much to do. We had many dedicated teachers. Prior to and during WW II, some of the teachers were: Maude Chase, Florence Shafer, E. J. Kretzinger, Doc Allensworth, G. L. Rader, Alta Shafer, Laura Stouffer, Gladys Cunningham, Casimer Newdome and Marie Fogle. Activities we enjoyed included the May Day pole dance, the Farmers' Institute, class plays, sporting events, and the Paulding County Fair. Skating parties at Ft. Brown were enjoyed by kids of all grades.

Walter May, a prominent banker, taught Sunday School at the U. B. Church for many years. Harley Shisler was very active in the U. B. Church. He would get groups from the surrounding area to put on programs which soon increased the attendance. Over time, the church had a change of preachers. My uncle Harold enjoyed Preacher's Howell's delivery. Preacher Risley and certain family members added a new dimension to church activities. Eddie Loomis was an exceptional preacher. He headed up the scouting program and was influential in the lives of many young men.

Oakwood also had a radio station. Call letters were WGDS which stood for Gerald and Delbert Shisler. It was not very powerful but could be heard though the town. It lasted for a few years.

Teeny's Jug Band was formed by Delbert Shisler. The band would play at area events and over WONW Ft. Wayne. Members were Delbert and Paul Shisler, Rudy Bray, Zeb Bell and Paul Ferris.

Each summer, Harry Shannon's tent show would come to town for a week. The cast put on stage plays. We were there when they arrived so we could help and earn free tickets. Also during the summer two medicine men came to town, set up on Main Street and hawked their wares. They had products that would cure, heal and invigorate your body. They were very entertaining.

Later on voters decided to join the Paulding school system instead of voting to build an addition to the high school. Doing so eliminated many of the activities enjoyed by the residents and soon the makeup of the town changed drastically. Business places closed, people moved away and not much remains of the Oakwood I once knew, but it was and will always be for me and many of my friends our home town.

Richard Harris

Van Wert, Ohio

Newton and Ida Hays

Newton and Ida Hays moved from Illinois to their newly purchased farmland north of Oakwood located on what is now road 209. They had

Newton Hays lifting sugar beets out of the ground with a beet lifter

Hungarian workers working in the sugar beet field

Loyal Hays with a load of sugar beets

five children: Loyal J. Hays, Letha Hays Thomas, Lola Hays Hamilton, Bonnie Hays Shisler, and Carrie Hays Blair.

One of the crops they raised on their farm was sugar beets. The first picture shows Newton Hays lifting sugar beets out of the ground with a beet lifter. The second picture is of laborers from Hungary which Newton hired to cut tops off of the sugar beets and put them in piles to be shoveled into a wagon. The third picture is Newton's son, Loyal Hays standing by a wagon with 4 ½ tons of sugar beets in it right before it was taken to the sugar beet processing factory in Paulding. These pictures were taken in October of 1927.

Lewis Heller

Lew R. Heller, 82-year old Melrose man who has done a lot of hunting in his day, and who learned to play the violin after 80, has a homespun philosophy for a long and happy life.

He says the secret is to put his left shoe on first each morning as he has done most of his life, and when you get up in the morning, make happiness your choice.

Lew, who has made a lot of friends, says "If you want to be happy, it is easy. When you get up in the morning you have two choices: Either to be happy or to be unhappy."

When you do the things Lew has done, you don't have time to grow old, he declared.

Lew was about two years old when his parents along with five brothers and three sisters moved in 1875 into the woods five miles north and a half mile east of Oakwood. There his father built a log cabin and Lew grew up playing with his brothers and sisters and helping clear the woods.

There were no lights, paved roads, ditches or any of what is now called modern conveniences. The family had a horse and wagons.

In 1895, Lew married his favorite girl, Miss Etta Hoover, with Rev. Henry Prowant, United Brethren pastor, performing the ceremony. They had a son who died at 13 months.

During the first year of married life, Lew farmed the home place with a team of horses, a plow and a drag. The farm is now owned by the Warner family. He recalls that it was possible to start farming on $200 capital.

Mr. Heller started to work for the light company in Defiance during his second year of married life. He trimmed wicks on carbon lights and filled street lights seven days a week. After four years on the job in Defiance, Lew with his brother Sam started to operate a threshing outfit. They continued this work for 16 years in the areas of Oakwood, Melrose, Arthur and Junction.

Next, Mr. Heller started another threshing machine with another brother, George, and continued this for seven years, for a total of 23 years in the harvesting business.

Mr. Heller then returned to farming the home place, but in two years bought the general store at Hartsburg from the late John Hosler who moved to Oakwood into the house where Orin Harris now resides. After a few years, he sold the Hartsburg store and purchased one at St. Joe, Ind., which he operated for three years, then sold it and took a job with the Ball Band company. After four years, he again returned to the home farm.

Mr. Heller went deer hunting to Maine Nov. 5, 1921, for the first time and returned for yearly hunting trips to that state for some time. He brought a total of 23 deer back from Maine. One time he hung two carcasses in front of Fruchey's store. The head of one now hangs in the post office. Lew gave one of the 239-pound animals to the lodge which used it for a free supper.

In later years, Mr. Heller moved to Melrose where he continues to make his home and where his wife died.

Mr. Heller does his own housework and not content to just grow old, he started a hobby of making Christmas card baskets when 80 years old. It takes 20 cards for one basket and 10 to 12 hours of work. He went to several hospitals and homes for the aged to show patients how to make the baskets. He did this good work without charge.

He also learned to play the violin when 80 years old. He now plays quite well for dances and his own enjoyment. Andy Nickels, who held the fiddling championship for Ohio, Indiana and Michigan, visits Lew often.

Lew had owned a fiddle for more than 50 years but "could not play a note." On one visit Andy said: "I will teach you to play the fiddle, so we can play together." In six weeks, Lew was playing the fiddle well.

Mr. Heller remembers the first lights, automobiles, trains, stoning of roads and many other changes. He is a member of the United Brethren Church.

Harley Shisler

Writing for the Defiance Crescent News March, 1955

Lester Hill

For many years, Lester and his wife Freda operated Hill's restaurant in Oakwood. However, they sold their business when Lester began to lose his sight. Several years after Lester lost his vision, he attended school at the State School for the Blind in Columbus, Ohio and learned the art of making brooms. It took him about five months to master the skill. Returning to Oakwood, he set up a broom making factory in his garage.

On the average, he would make 12 to 18 brooms a day. He made five different types of brooms. His wife Freda assisted with the business by delivering orders, keeping the books and taking orders.

Mr. and Mrs. Hill were the parents of four children: Errol, Imogene Risley, Anson and John Mark. Both Anson and John Mark served as missionaries.

E & N Honda Center / The Honda Center

E & N Honda Center was started in 1964 by Ronald Ehrman and Walter J. Noffsinger. They rented Harold Shisler's Slaughter House on South First Street, Oakwood, Ohio. After much shoveling and scrapping the walls, the building was painted a bright blue, inside and out.

At the time there were no Honda Motorcycle dealers in the area. American Honda Motor Company's theme to fame was: "You meet the Nicest People on a Honda". Many people had never heard the name Honda. To be able to be a dealer, you had to buy ten (10) motorcycles. The sizes ranged from a 50cc to 305cc motorcycles. The first ten motorcycles were quickly sold and the dealership was well on its way. Faye Ehrman and Shelby Jean Noffsinger managed the office, parts and accessories. Ronnie and Walter were the mechanics. As business increased, many local boys and men helped out part time. Motorcycles were becoming quite popular, so they took on the dealership for Royal Enfield Motorcycles.

Business was growing and the American Honda Motor Company wanted a dealership in Defiance, so in 1968 the decision was made to move the business to Defiance on Hopkins Street. At that time, Yamaha and Triumph Motorcycles were added to the dealership. As time went on, Walter bought out Ronnie and the business was soon moved to a larger location on Spruce Street behind S&K Tool.

The business continued to grow and a final move was made to a new building on State Route 66, north of Defiance. Snowmobiles were the going winter sport, so Polaris snowmobiles were added to the recreation line. They were employing 10 people full and part time.

Walter had continued to farm and Shelby Jean managed the business. Due to Shelby's health, it was decided to slow down and sell the business. McCarthy Yamaha purchased the business and is still operating it today.

Submitted by Walter and Shelby Jean Noffsinger

George Hornish

This is your life: George was born in Defiance County, his parents being John Hornish the II and Eva (Treece) Hornish. Your mother was born in Munich, Germany and came to the United States in 1846 and was married to John Hornish II the same year.

Your father was a loyal church worker and minister and was admired by all in the community in which he lived. Twelve children were born to this family, of which George was the eighth child. In those pioneer days the main thought was food for the large family. Eight or ten hogs were butchered each year and the meat was put down in a salt brine. Bread and pies were baked in an outdoor oven.

George's grandfather, John Hornish I, was one of the first five families who settled in Adams Township, Defiance County. After his marriage to Amanda Hane in 1885, they lived in Defiance County until 1893. They then came to Paulding County to make their home in Brown Twp.; on the farm where George still resides. He purchased these 160 acres at $40.00 per acre. You took great pride in farming and kept your land up so at the present time it is worth approximately $400.00 per acre.

Death darkened your doors twice, the first being in 1924 when Wilma, at the age of 19 years, passed away suddenly, three days before commencement. Her senior classmates had charge of the funeral which was held at the Arthur Church on the day of the graduation exercises.

Jay. M. Reed, Superintendent of the Oakwood High School at that time, assisted with the funeral.

Death came a second time to your home, when your wife passed away seven years ago. For the past three years, your niece, Berthat Lehman, has kept your home for you.

You and one sister, Nancy Lehman of Defiance, are the only two left of the large family of 12 children. You still enjoy talking about the old political days. The first president you voted for was Grover Cleveland.

Your first car was a Model T Ford purchased in 1910 and it was a stem wind. You joined the Church of the Brethren at Dupont in 1918, and have served as a trustee and various other officers of this church, of which you are still a member.

You and Graff Shisler helped to start the telephone line north of Oakwood. You have also served on the Board of Education, Township Trustee, the Telephone Board and for a number of years was a land appraiser.

Harley Shisler

Writing for the Oakwood News June 1955

Hotel Walters

With no fanfare, the house on Auglaize Street at the end of West Harmon Street was demolished this summer – no evidence is left of what was once a special place in Oakwood, Ohio. Let me tell you about it.

My Great Grandfather Wilson Abraham Walters (Wils) constructed the building around 1885 to house a hotel which his wife, Elizabeth Frances (Lib) managed; it was also the home for their daughter, Anna (Ritchie) age 9 and John age 6. Frank and Ella Hakes, plus two hired girls were employed to do the work at the Hotel.

The Hotel Walters: O. S. Ritchie, Anna Ritchie, Elizabeth
Walters, Ella Hakes, Wilson Walters and Colley the horse

Fresh produce for the Hotel plus enough for the help to can and preserve for the winter was grown by Wils on two acres of land owned by the Walters family, located where the Oakwood Ball Park is now. The help also butchered much of the meat for the Hotel dining room. Wils had a cow for milk and a horse on this property, as well.

The over-night guests were mostly food and merchandise salesmen who came in on the Nickel Plate passenger train. They usually came on a regular schedule and Lib would make sure their favorite meals would be served. A number of local businessmen also ate at the Hotel.

A lot of fine linens and China were collected for the Hotel during Lib's many travels – by train in those days. She took in the Louisiana Purchase Exposition in St. Louis in 1904. Traveled to Texas and Mexico in 1909 and visited Washington DC that same year. Many trend setting ideas must have been brought back to Oakwood from her travels. We do know that she persuaded her local grocer to bring the first grapefruit to Oakwood.

The Hotel finances were managed by Lib and any spare money was put into real estate. The Hotel was rented to Ella Hakes in 1910 and the Walters moved to a house on First Street (not still standing) until Lib and a carpenter from Cloverdale finished their home next door to the Hotel.

The 1913 flood caused major damage to all five of the Walter's properties. Lib was visiting her son in Texas and got back as the waters were receding. The stress was too much for her; she lost her mind (thought to be caused by a blood clot on her brain) and died in 1920 at a State Hospital in Toledo. She is buried in Prairie Chapel Cemetery.

I do not know if the hotel reopened after the flood. At some point, Wils moved into an apartment of three rooms on the north side of the Hotel. (The rest of the building was furnished but not occupied in my memory.) Raisins and peanuts were always on Grandpa Walters' kitchen table as he thought they were good for you. We kids thought so, too. He walked four miles every morning. His winters were spent in Houston, Texas with his son and family where he died in January 1939 at the age of 93. He is buried in Prairie Chapel Cemetery.

The Hotel property became the home of Sam and Alta Mead and their son Joe. Sam died in 1975 but Alta continued to live in the house until her death in 1979. After that the house passed through a number of hands, was poorly maintained and trashed by renters. After standing vacant for a number of years, it sadly had to be demolished in the summer of 2013. There is left a lovely grass space with mature trees and a view of the beautiful Auglaize River.

Submitted by Helen Maddock

Foy Kohler 1908 - 1990

Foy Kohler was the son of David and Myrtle McClure Kohler. He was born in Oakwood and at one time his father had a photography business in the old telephone building.

His parents left Oakwood when Foy was five years old, moving first to McComb, Ohio and then to Toledo, Ohio. Foy graduated from Scott High School, Toledo at the age of 16. He then attended Toledo University and Ohio State University, graduating from Ohio State in 1931. Following graduation, he joined the State Department's diplomatic corps. Over the years, he served in posts in Canada, Yugoslavia, Romania, Greece, Egypt, Vietnam, Bolivia and the Soviet Union.

In 1962, President John F. Kennedy named him Ambassador to the Soviet Union. He served there during the Cuban Missile Crisis and during the defection of Joseph Stalin's daughter to the United States.

He retired in 1967 with the rank of Career Ambassador. Following his retirement, he and his wife, Phyllis, moved to Florida where he taught at the University of Miami.

Foy Kohler

Memories of Emery and Mabel Kretzinger

Emery was one of seven children born near to Oakwood to Henry Burtnett Kretzinger and Charlotte Ann Bidlack. He helped with the family farm and attended country schools. Eventually he went to college in Ada, Bowling Green and Defiance where he graduated in 1932.

On June 22, 1912, he married Mabel and they were the parents of three girls—Hazel born in 1913, Helen born in 1914 and Audrey born in 1915. Grandma always described their close births as bang, bang, bang.

I don't really have any stories to share about my grandfather. He died when I was 17 and for several years before that he was bedfast unable to speak. His health started to deteriorate in the 50's and he was diagnosed with hardening of the arteries. I do remember that he always had a stash of white and pink peppermints in a cupboard for when he had a sour taste in his mouth. I do know he loved learning and had a special interest in history and poetry since he had a collection of books on those subjects. He taught school for several years and was superintendent at Oakwood. He retired in 1947. He did some carpentry and I have a small plant stand and doll bed he made. The bed is being prepared to pass on to his great-great granddaughter.

Mabel was the daughter of John and Anna Badman. She was born in Putnam Co. near Kieferville. She had one brother, Scott Badman, and one half-sister, Viola Fuller.

She always had an apron close at hand and always wore one while working. And she did work. She always had cookies in the jar that set on top of the refrigerator just waiting for company to arrive. She often made noodles and, to this day, I haven't tasted noodles as good as grandma made.

I don't think anyone would dispute me if I said that grandma was conservative. The grandchildren could relate story after story describing grandma's frugality. The last house she occupied had one bathroom but it was upstairs. Many times my mother and Aunt Hazel suggested having a bath put in downstairs but Grandma would have nothing to do with that idea. If she didn't want to climb the stairs she would make do with the outside john which was attached to the back of her house. She may have wished that she hadn't used this facility the day she pulled her pants down only to be attacked by yellow jackets. As I recall she didn't take the time to pull her undies up but since she never wore slacks, her dress did preserve her modesty as she hastily left the outhouse.

Grandma loved to chew Juicy Fruit and Black Jack gum. But one chewing was not enough. One could usually find a wad of gum resting on the table ready to be chewed again. Re-chewing gum even became apparent to Pauline Shisler who lived across the street and visited often usually bearing a package of gum. She even brought a tiny ceramic hand to hold grandma's cud when not in use.

The IRS was never grandma's friend. She really hated giving her money to the government. She got in the habit of calling them the "Infernal" Revenue Service. This gave us all a laugh when she reported that she mistakenly wrote a check made out to the Infernal Revenue. I imagine she really was disheartened to tear up that check and start over.

Pennies were also pinched when it came to fuel oil. A large stove sat in one of the rooms and we discovered that if she got cold she would somehow hoist herself up to sit on top of this stove. Had not someone seen her through the big window as they were on the porch I don't think we would have ever been aware of this.

The only alcohol in grandma's house was rubbing alcohol. And there was never a deck of cards to be played. Both were sure to lead to moral degradation. My mother used to say that she was reluctantly allowed to square dance but never round dance. Heaven only knows what dancing in the arms of a man would lead to. Wonder what grandma would think of Dancing with the Stars and the skimpy costumes and suggestive moves.

And speaking of television, grandma never would buy herself one and would have never had one except the girls bought one for her at Christmas one year. I am happy to report that she spent many hours watching it.

To my knowledge grandma never bought new furniture. I rocked many an hour in rockers that were in the house for as long as I could remember. She did get a sofa and chair from an estate sale.

Grandma's life was far from easy but I never heard her complain. Her middle daughter, Helen, died unexpectedly at the age of 13. As the girls were preparing to return to school after Christmas break, Helen collapsed while coming downstairs. Granddad tried to resuscitate her but to no avail. She is also buried here. Her mother lived with them the last years of her life and of course there was the care of granddad. It would not have entered grandma's mind to have put him in a nursing home. And that was her biggest fear during the last years of her life. She told all of us that she did not want to go to a home. Thankfully, she never had to face that since she died quietly in her home. It appeared that grandma had gotten up and had dressed but hadn't unlocked her doors. She apparently stretched out on the sofa, fell asleep and never woke up.

There was little money during the early years of her marriage. I'm sure this is what led her to be so frugal.

Grandma loved company and when you dropped in you had better be prepared to stay. I am certain that she woke up in the morning and thought of something she could call a daughter or grandchild to come and do. She would always say there was no hurry but that, I soon learned, was code for I'll give you 5 minutes to come before I call you again. Stuart remembers the time when grandma wanted him to clean her eave spouts over her porch. He had to climb through an upstairs window. He no more than got started when he turned around and there was grandma supervising. My job was to trim the hedges which nearly surrounded the house. Grandma was quick to point out one little twig if it stuck above the others. That hedge had to be perfectly flat on top.

Grandma was a great influence on many lives and I have to say that I am the person I am today, in part, as a result of Grandma's being such a wonderful role model.

By their granddaughter Karen Jacobs

At a cemetery walk September 2013

Mr. Kretzinger

Mr. Kretzinger was the superintendent during my twelve years of school at Oakwood. He was considered to be a most qualified and good man. I always believed him to be a man of great knowledge. I can see him, in mind's eye, standing in front of the study hall, reciting great poetry of great length, which made a great impression me.

My first two years of teaching were under his supervision. It was during war time. Many qualified teachers were in the service. I didn't believe I could do the job, since had only one year of college, but he had faith in me – besides, schools were desperate for teachers. In his quiet, but confident way, he encouraged me to make the teaching of children my way of life.

Submitted by Kathryn Sharp Deatrick

Dr. Frank Leatherman

My "Pop" was Dr. Leatherman. He like to garden. He had been raised on the farm and that was still part of him. The habit of marking the line between stakes by which to put in the seeds or plants was the way he had been taught to make a garden. He was always very particular about having nice, straight rows. His thing was to have nice straight rows and to make sure the rows were about 18 inches apart

Submitted by Evalena Sharp Fitzwater

My Pop: He was Dr. I. F. Leatherman, but most people called him Doc, but I called him Pop. There are so many things that could be written about him and so I will. He was the kindest man I have ever known and was a good, decent man. As a child I rode many times with him on what he called his "drives", which meant he was going to someone's farm to care for a sick animal. His medical office was in the front room of the large barn on our property. He would take care of dogs and cats there.

If the animal was to be spayed/neutered, he would tell me I needed to go to the house.

Being nosey, especially as a little girl, I was there as much as I could. I thought his work seemed really interesting, so I was a real pest I guess, asking questions about the animals, their sickness and the medicines.

He often told us about the sicknesses of animals and his work with them. Often times during the late 20's and early 30's – depression era – he would not receive any money from the farmers for his trips or medicine to doctor the animals but some would give him baked goods or something they would have – but money was hard to "come by" for everyone during that time.

One time he was seriously hurt when he had gone to a farm to castrate a horse. The horse did not agree with what he was doing so proceeded to start kicking and shoving. My grandpa was shoved into the side of the stall. Before he could be rescued he had several serious injuries – a broken collar bone, broken ribs, a broken leg and many bruises. With all of this, he gathered up his "tools", got in the car and drove home. When arriving there he blew his horn but nobody came. We were all busy having supper and didn't hear the sound, so he proceeded to get out of the car and hobble as best he could to the door and pounded on it to get our attention. What a sight! The doctor was called. Since he was past middle-age the healing took a long time

Submitted by Kathryn Sharp Deatrick

Dr. Frank Leatherman, veterinarian, has lived in the vicinity of Oakwood most of his life and has doctored pets and livestock in nearly every part of Paulding and Putnam Counties. Since he has not limited calls to any particular area, he has treated animals as far south as Spencerville, in Allen County, and also has gone into Michigan.

He still drives his own car on calls whenever the weather permits, although he now refuses to go on a case late at night. He does not intend to retire, and he certainly appears capable of continuing his profession another decade.

Although he is slight in stature, he is stong in will, so he has overcome several serious illnesses and a number of accidents, caused from his handling of livestock.

Dr. Leatherman cannot only remember Oakwood from its years of beginning in the pre-railroad days, but he recalls many small towns along the Miami-Erie Canal that later became ghost towns.

Dr. Frank Leatherman

Frank Leatherman, better known as I. F., was born in 1871; he was one of fifteen children. His parents, Hiram and Catherine (Shafer) Leatherman, came from Putnam to Paulding County during the Civil War. Previous to that time, his grandfather, Michael Leatherman and the Shafer's, who had come from Pennsylvania, lived in Allen County, northeast of Lima. The Shafer's home was on land which now is the site of the State Hospital for the Criminally Insane. Three of his sisters married the Matson brothers: John, William, and Israel.

The Hiram Leathermans settled in Paulding County along the canal bank south of Oakwood, near the little village of Murat. Here Frank attended the Knox School. In speaking of the town of Murat, Dr. Leatherman said: "A Mr. Edwards had a store there where he sold everything from groceries to hardware and liquor. He had a brother in business, too. The fellows called him 'Gum'."

Later the Leathermans moved down the canal toward Ottoville south of Mandale. This was near the Antioch Church of God which still stands. Although near the Van Wert County line, it was in Paulding County, and they had to go to Paulding Center to pay taxes. During the winter of 1896, the weather was bad. Travel by any means was nearly impossible except for Frank. He often skimmed on skates over the ice of the canal. He skated as far as Charloe, removed his skates, rested awhile and then followed the creeks and lowlands that were covered by ice, to Paulding where he handed the treasurer his tax money. When the official saw the location of the property, he asked: "How in the world did you get over here?" "I skated."

Not only did Dr. Leatherman skate upon the canal, he swam, boated and fished in it as well. For a while he even tended "Dead Man's Lock", south of Mandale. The lock was thus named because a Mr. Goodwin had killed a man there where the two fellows had lived together in a shanty. The other man returned from Ottoville terribly drunk. When Goodwin would not let him in, he battered the door down with a rail, attacked Goodwin, who to protect himself, grabbed an ax, and in his rage did more than a rail-splitting job. Anyhow his assailant was dead when neighbors found him.

"The locks", Dr. Leatherman explained, "were necessary to change the level of the water so that incoming boats had to stop until the locks were filled. Then the gate would be opened and the boats could pass through. Boats coming from the opposite direction waited for the lock to be emptied or lowered. The water entered and left the locks through wickets. It was necessary to have someone adjust the lock to the direction of the boat. The mule driver usually did this opening and closing the locks whenever there was no tender, but often we boys, who were sitting along the bank, would do it for him. Then we were usually invited to ride to the next town. We would either wait for the next boat back or walk home along the canal. When we were asked to ride on the steam packet, we would think we had had a real treat. The steam packet went from Royal Oak to Defiance one day, and the next day it went to Delphos."

After several years of farming, Frank decided to become a veterinarian, which required more than his elementary schooling, so he attended part of a term at Dupont. Then he enrolled at Normal School at Middlepoint College near the Ridge east of Van Wert. Nothing remains but the ruins of this college which was quite a place in its day.

Dr. T. P. Fast, Grover Hill physician, attended Middlepoint College at the same time. The two young men were close friends and played ball together. According to the tales Dr. Leatherman tells, Middlepoint College had many characteristics of modern campus life.

Frank Leatherman was 39 years old and had been out of school 17 years when he finally took his first veterinary training at Grand Rapids, Michigan. He left there with credit for 100 semester hours work and finished his training in veterinary science and education at Cincinnati. Veterinary colleges no longer exist at these places but at that time, these government maintained schools gave him a degree equal to one received in the largest universities.

In 1889, he married Eva Shafer (no relation). She was the daughter of Jefferson and Mary Ann (Prowant) Shafer. Their only child was a daughter, now Mrs. Faye Sharp, who lives with her father. Mrs. Sharp's children are: Mrs. Walter (Evalena) Fitzwater, Mrs. John (Kathryn) Deatrick, and Ned Sharp, all of Oakwood; Harry Sharp, Albany, Georgia, and Mrs. Charles (LuAnn) Collins, Indianapolis.

In 1901, Mr. Leatherman was elected treasurer of Washington Township and served two terms. He said that Mr. Wagner, Mandale storekeeper, helped him campaign. Mr. Leatherman was one of five men who were responsible for the organization of the Oakwood Mutual Telephone system in 1916. He has served many times as a director.

Since coming to Oakwood a half a century ago, Dr. Leatherman has served several times on the school board and many times on the town council. He has always been active in church and community affairs and has been a member of The Dupont Church of the Brethren since joining in 1903. He is the oldest member of the Northwestern Ohio Veterinary Association and probably one of the oldest ones in the state.

It was in his home that Miss Maud Chase, Oakwood home economics and Latin teacher lived for 26 years, a longer period of time than any other teacher had been in the school system. Miss Chase now teaches vocational economics at Jewell and lives in her own home.

Dr. Leatherman is now apparently in excellent health. However, he was very ill with the flu in 1918, had typhoid fever twice, has had a stroke of paralysis, and was nearly blind for a week. He has suffered accidents while treating livestock and dogs. His leg was broken by a fallen horse, once a rib was broken, another time he had both collar bones broken, and the flesh the length of his forearm was torn by an angry German police dog. He said that the dog's claws cut through like razor blades.

He has worn out 17 automobiles since the time he drove horses. He tells interesting experiences of the horse and buggy days. He kept two horses and changed them when one was tired. Sometimes he drove as far as 75 miles a day. "I had driven up the river one time to Cascade," he said, "and half way to Glandorf, when I returned home about 3 o'clock in the morning. I found a call wanting me to return to Cascade, so I hitched a fresh horse to the buggy. It was raining and the roads were muddy. The wheels of the buggy sank so deep that I had to take a spade and dig them out from the mud." "In those days," he remarked, "I slept in the daytime and made calls during the night. I don't know why it was, but animals always seem to get ill at night. At least, that is when folks always called me."

What with flat tires and running out of gas, automobiles were not much better in the early days before there was a filling station on every corner. "I used to always be dead on my feet," he added, "since people then gave me little rest."

In more recent years, since there are younger veterinarians, Dr. Leatherman has rested more. Since his wife's death he and his daughter have taken several trips together. They visited Florida in 1940 and lived for three weeks in a trailer. Later when he visited his great nephew, who farms 1100 acres of the King ranch in Texas, they went to Mexico. Dr. Leatherman enjoyed his visit to the King 70-mile square ranch, supposed to be the largest ranch in the world. There he saw many kinds of animals as well as livestock and observed different methods of farming. "Onions were planted like corn," he said, "and before they were harvested, cotton was planted between the rows, so that a double crop could be reaped each season."

He and his daughter, Faye, have made an interesting hobby of growing prize dahlias on highly fertilized, heavily watered soil under the cover of a thin cloth enclosure so no insect could mar their large blooms. People drove for miles to see this beautiful display, but found creeping under the cloth cover a hot experience. At one time, they had more than 150 varieties and had hundreds of plants and bulbs. The work of caring for them became too heavy, so Dr. Leatherman stopped raising them several years ago.

Based on an article in the Defiance Crescent News February 1961

Dean Lighthill

During his life, Dean lived in Oakwood and Grover Hill. He operated a photography studio in Oakwood for several years and has left us a priceless legacy of pictures that he took of Oakwood including many that he took during the 1913 flood. His studio was located in a building that stood about where the Legion building is now. His son in law,

Carson Eakins often joked that Dean was out taking pictures during the flood (instead of saving his possessions from the rising flood waters) and when the flood was over, all he had was the camera he had with him and the clothes he was wearing. The building containing his studio was destroyed.

Dean Lighthill with his camera

Looking east on Harmon Street

The Oakwood Depot

Mormon's Tile Mill

The Oakwood Lions Club

The Oakwood Lions Club was re-chartered in about 1954. A banquet to celebrate the event was held at the high school gym and approximately 125 people were in attendance.

Charter members of the group were: Don Adams, Harold Adams, Robert Christy, Don Clemens, J. Tide Cook, Virgil Cooper, Melford Deatrick, George Dobbelaere, Victor Dunlap, Carleton Ehrman, Charles Estle, Harry Flechtner, Orlando Foust, Kenneth Gartrell, Gene Givens, Carl Guyton, Louis Herman, Stanley Howell, Archie Huff, Jr., William Huff, Clark C. Mead, Richard Miller, Ira Mohr, Richard Parrish, James Punches, Forest Penner, Darhl Roberts, Bill Robnolte, Dale Roughton, Raymond Roughton Jr., Harley Shisler, Lester Shisler, Logan Randolph, Richard Rickels, Ray Rickner, Albert Shafer, Lester Sherry, Harold Shisler, George Specht, Glenn Spencer, Arthur Staley, Donald Stephens, Don Weisenberger, Earl White, Deak Williams, Floyd Young, Ray Miller, Karl Adams, Allen Carnahan, Clyde Buchanan, Clifford Peck, Ned Schultz and Odey Mumy.

The local organization was very active in community affairs and sponsored a junior boys baseball team. They were instrumental in bringing Dr. Movchan to the community. They also raised money for various community needs including new uniforms for the high school band and toys for needy children at Christmas.

Walter C. and Effa May

They were married in 1905. Before their marriage, Effa worked in Fred Fender's store in Continental. At the time of their marriage, Walter was teaching school in the old school building in Oakwood. He taught the 7th and 8th grades. Lee Chalfant was the school superintendent at that time. Walter had also taught at the Fairview school east of Oakwood.

Walter served as Deputy Recorder at the Courthouse in Paulding when Frank Michael was the recorder. In 1913, they moved to Stanton, Michigan for a few years. Returning to Paulding County, they lived in Paulding where Walter again taught school for 19 months.

Effective, January 1, 1916 the directors of the Oakwood Deposit Bank hired Walter as cashier. He remained with the bank until his retirement becoming president of the bank in 1931. Effa also worked in the bank as the cashier.

Both Walter and Effa were active in the EUB Church in Oakwood. Walter served as Sunday School Superintendent for 25 years and they both taught Sunday School classes.

Walter's hobbies were history and reading. He was a member of the I.O.O.F. Lodge for over 50 years and also a member of the Freemasons. He served several terms on the Oakwood Village Council.

Effie loved to read and raise flowers.

Jeanne Bennett Calvert

Carl and Edith Peckhart Merriman

Carl and Edith Merriman were known as Pop and Mom to all the grandchildren. Carl Freeman Merriman was born in Fort Wayne, Indiana, on June 5, 1885. Edith Lydia Peckhart was born in Auburn, Indiana on February 24, 1895. Carl and Edith were married on February 27, 1912.

They had a total of ten children, but two were lost at childbirth. Their children were: Edward Merriman, Hilda Merriman Geren, Emma Merriman Porter, Leo Merriman and Bruce Merriman were the first five. In 1925, they moved to Paulding County, Ohio. They had three more children: Georgia Merriman Geren, Merle Merriman and Jean Merriman Britsch. Their children attended several different schools in the Paulding County area. Three of their sons, Edward, Leo and Merle were in the military during World War II and the Korean Conflict. Edith and her daughters wrote letters to the boys overseas keeping them informed about what was going on at home. One of the sons, Edward was taken as a prisoner during the Battle of the Bulge in Germany during World War II. After the war he came home to Florida for rehabilitation before returning home to the family.

Carl moved his family several times while in the Oakwood area. They lived at Rabies place on Seven Hills Road; Holmes Place, south of Oakwood and Thrashers place, north of Oakwood on Road 128. In 1965, they moved into a home next to Junior and Wilma Fohner's place, north of Oakwood on Route 66. This was the first place where they lived that they had indoor plumbing and it was their final residence.

Edith sewed many quilts that she shared with her children, grandchildren, great-grandchildren and great-great grandchildren. She enjoyed raising flowers and throughout the years she would take bouquets of flowers to her church, the Auglaize Chapel Church of God on Sundays. She would put the flowers in cans covered with aluminum foil. She also raised ducks, geese and chickens, which was a source of meat and eggs for the family.

Edith and Carl always invited their family home for dinner on Sundays, giving their children and grandchildren many fond memories. The food was homemade and tasted great. The holiday meals consisted of duck, chicken and noodles, and goose (we never heard of turkey). We had mashed potatoes, potato salad, jell-o, fruit pies, chocolate pie and

Edith, Age 16

Edith, Carl and Bruce

pumpkin pies. Everyone would bring a special dish to share.

Some of the places where they lived were a quarter to a half mile off the main road. On Thanksgiving and Christmas, cars would typically get stuck in the lane if it had rained or snowed because the lanes were packed dirt. The guys would get together to push the cars out. At times we had to walk from the road if the lane was snowbound or muddy.

When they lived on the Holmes Place south of Oakwood, along the river, Carl did a little farming. They had apple orchards and barnyard animals. Their barnyard and around the house were fenced in and Carl would leave his draft horses in the area to eat grass. Sometimes the horses would get to running around and you would think they were going to run over you. The outhouse was along the river behind the house, so when we went out, you took a chance that the gander would run after you and bite you. There was a spring along the river where they would get their drinking water.

Carl retired from the Nickel Plate Railroad after working several years. He also did blacksmithing, tended livestock, grew fruit trees and planted a garden. In 1999 Edith was in the Oakwood Labor Day Parade, she was an Honored Citizen and was 105 years old at the time.

Carl and Edith celebrated 63 years together. Carl died in 1973 at 88 years of age. Edith died in the year 2000 at 106 years of age. They are buried at the Little Auglaize Cemetery, south of Melrose, Ohio.

Flora Jean Porter Welch, Sherwood, Ohio
and Wilma Marie Porter Fohner, Oakwood

Carl and Edith on their 50th

Anniversary 1962

Money Issues

Following the defeat of an operating levy in November 1956, the entire village council at the time resigned. Their final act was to dismiss the town marshal and village maintenance worker as there was no money to pay them. They also closed the Town Hall as there was no one to clean it.

Mayor Harley Shisler called a meeting of the village residents to discuss possible solutions to the problem. One of the suggestions was for the village to un-incorporate and be under the township governing body. There was little enthusiasm for this idea.

Mayor Shisler appointed six new councilmen to deal with the problems. They were: Don (Enie) Weisenburger, L. E. Speakman, Todd Roughton, Ira Mohr, Ralph Cooper and Donald Stevens.

In the meantime, several citizens volunteered their time and services to carry out some of the maintenance and cleaning functions of the village employee.

Henry Matson

Pictured above is Henry Matson at the Oakwood Produce Company. (The exact location of the building and the date of the photo are unknown.) Henry is the great-grandfather of the late Imogene (Tracy) Moore.

Bruce and Imogene Moore

My parents, Bruce and Imogene Moore purchased their home on East Harmon Street on May 5, 1955, and lived there until their passing in 2008 and 1996, respectively. All my memories of Oakwood are good ones. While there was no mall, theater or swimming pool it seemed like there was never a lack of things to do. Oakwood did have Ott's IGA, and for a time, the department store in the basement, Risley's Rexall Drug Store and the S & S Locker. (Remember the hanging beef in the cooler which was almost as fascinating as the candy counter?)

It seems like our family spent a great deal of time at Oakwood High School with various events. Brother Robert played basketball, sister Linda was a cheerleader. Although the size of the gym there was miniscule by today's standards, the home Varsity and Reserve Oakwood Bobcat basketball games were monumental in spirit and community pride. To feel the bleachers vibrating and cheering so loud it was deafening was wonderful. And to finally be of age to sit on the stage with the student body cheering section was certainly a childhood rite of passage. Band and choir concerts, the WOWO Penny Pitch and WOWO Air Aces basketball games were all such good memories.

The annual school fall festival was such a fun event. While younger kids enjoyed winning goldfish at one of the many booths in the gym, the record hop was being held upstairs in the band room, the "General Store" located in the Industrial Arts room, where free puppies and Ed Stover's homemade wooden barns were big hits.

Who could ever forget the terrific school lunches prepared by Mary Lois Kohart, Ethel Adams and Virginia Brown? I honestly do not believe I have had peanut butter cookies that delicious since. I've often thought that those ladies should have made up a recipe book to hand out to each child that attended there. It was with much sadness that Auglaize-Brown Local/Oakwood High School ceased before my high school and graduation year arrived. Laura Speakman was my third grade teacher, as she had taught my older brother and sister. I do not believe Mrs. Speakman ever used my name the whole school year, always calling me Linda, and sometimes even Robert.

While the school and churches seemed to be at the center of the Oakwood community, it truly was the residents there that were the heart and soul of it. It seemed as if everyone knew everyone else, their parents and children and relation. While some may think this was intrusive, I always felt it to be comforting. It is wonderful to have multi generations of the same family remain in the same town. Presently, the third generation of the Moore family is residing in the same house on Harmon Street. These are the heartfelt ties that bind one to their hometown, roots and a sense of continuity.

Linda, Robert, Imogene, Patricia, Bruce Moore

On a Saturday morning in mid-December of 1966, we had a house fire. While only one room actually suffered fire damage, water and smoke damage filtered into every corner. Our mishap was announced at the home basketball game that night and early on Sunday morning, many members of the Oakwood community arrived with buckets and rags and covered dishes of food. With just a week to go before Christmas, we were able to be back in our home, due to the caring and helping hand generosity of a community that I feel remains to this day.

Submitted by Patricia Moore Vance

Paulding, Ohio

Andy Nickels: This is your life

You are now 66 years old and still love to play your fiddle and banjo. You started to play at home at the age of five years. Your father, Calvin Nickels, who was a school teacher and band leader, taught you how to play and when you were 8 you started to fiddle the violin. You have played in five states, on the radio and for a lot of dances and stage shows. You are the happiest when you can play for some one. I can remember when you played at Indian Village with the late Geo. Royce.

You won your first trophy in an old time fiddlers contest in 1952. You are a trick fiddler and make both young and old laugh. Your fiddle is 90 years old and still plays like a new one. You have the only 8-string violin that I know of in this part of the country. You made it yourself in 1933; it took most of three years to do the job. You made it out of pine and your tools were a pocket knife and a piece of glass.

After the death of your wife, you lived alone and did your own housework. At one time you had your own family band. However, all the kids married and moved away, so this left Andy and his fiddle to start all over again.

You play each year at the Pumpkin Show at Bradner, O., and this year will be your 17th straight appearance there.

You still have five children living. When I asked Andy what his hobby was, he said, "fiddling" of course."

Nearly everyone has heard Andy play if not, you can go to his home at Melrose and he'll be more than happy to "give out with some good old hoe-down music."

Here's hoping that Andy will live to a ripe old age. When he gets down in the dumps he gets his fiddle out and forgets his troubles with music.

"You never get too old to learn to play the violin," Andy says. He added "I taught Lewis Heller to play when he was 80 years old."

Harley Shisler

Writing for the Oakwood News

Walter and Hilda Noffsinger

Walter Samuel Noffsinger and Hilda Charlotte (Rhees) Noffsinger lived their married life on the Paulding-Putnam County Line Road, being on the Paulding County side.

Walter Noffsinger

Hilda Noffsinger

Walter and Hilda were both elementary school teachers. They had taught at various schools in Paulding and Putnam Counties before coming to the Melrose School. Walter was the Superintendent there for many years and Hilda taught the first and second grades.

Walter was the son of John and Mae (Shafer) Noffsinger. Hilda was the daughter of Edgar and Mina (Kretzinger) Rhees. They were the parents of four sons: Walter John Noffsinger, Waldo Edgar Noffsinger who died in 1937, Noland Dana Noffsinger and Leland Noffsinger.

Walter John married Shelby Jean Barnes and they had three children: Lynn Alan, Rhonda Lee and Colette Marie. They reside in Monroe Township, Putnam County, Ohio.

Wedding Day   Shelby Jean and Walter

Noland married Charlotte Andrews and they had two children: Brent and Angie. They live in Littleton, Colorado.

Leland married Doris Warncke from Defiance. Their children are: Denise, Ranae and Michelle. Leland and Doris reside on the Putnam County side of the Paulding-Putnam County Line Road.

Submitted by Walter and Shelby Noffsinger

Jerrolyn Bradford Parrott remembers:

When I started walking down memory lane there were so many things that were, that will never be again, sometimes, thank goodness, sometimes it would be nice to bring back the experience.

I remember going with my dad Ralph (Johnny) Bradford to get cow or pig feed. We would hook up the trailer to the car (few people at that time had more than 1 vehicle) get the sacks and go to the feed mill located north of the railroad on 2nd street. I remember the floor being so smooth where they moved the filled sacks to the loading area. Back home we would go to unload feed.

We would sometimes stop at Deak's Café owned by my dad's uncle Deak Williams. It was located in part of what is now the Landing Strip. Dad really enjoyed taking us kids with him.

Then there was the Oakwood Elevator which was quite a busy place. The Elevator not only bought grain they sold all kinds of things just like a general store. Violet "Ruthie" Bodenbender and Sharon Boohner were bookkeepers over the years.

My mother, Eunice (Carnahan) Bradford was way too patient with me. She had one way to do things, the right way. I had to complete many chores more than once to meet her satisfaction. I was a member of the Brown Betty's 4-H club, later named Brown Betty's and Buster Brown 4-H Club, which is still an active 4-H Club today. Again, mom, who was an advisor still had to have things done the right way. I remember making a black velvet dress. I don't know how many times I would throw the thing in the corner because I was going to have to redo something. Mom would say "Go outside, cool off, come in and start over." And I did. Thanks to her patient guidance I usually qualified for the Ohio State Fair. In many situations she should have used a ball bat on me, because I know now that I was not very co-operative.

Mom was a charter member of the Everwilling Club organized in 1948. It still meets the 4th Thursday of most months.

As a teenager, I remember how important the Oakwood Bobcat basketball season was a community pride and joy.

The Oakwood ball park (Badman Field) has many memories of my kids and grandkids learning the game. Thanks to the many people over the years that have donated countless hours, keeping the Oakwood Ball Park operating.

We were far from rich but we were taught the value of the dollar, to save, to be a good neighbor and give back to our community. That is the best memory of all.

My mother, Eunice Carnahan Bradford was always able to laugh at situations she got herself into. When she was 80 years old she purchased a new mattress set. The store called, told her they would deliver the mattress set in a few minutes. Shortly after the telephone call, the door bell sounded. She answered the door and was surprised the delivery person was so prompt, and told him she was surprised to see him so soon. She said "Would you like to look at my bedroom?" The delivery man made no response. Again she asked the man to follow her to her bedroom. Again no response. She looked at his shirt. It was the Schwann man. He never stopped at her house again. She did get her new mattress set.

Plumb's Crossroads

Plumb's Crossroad was a small village located three miles southeast of Roselms. It has disappeared like many other small villages in the area.

At one time, it had a store, a sawmill, some houses and a post office. The Plumb family who gave the area their name, operated a sawmill in the village. Caleb Plumb built the store and his wife started the first Sunday School in Washington Township. It later grew into the Mellinger Methodist Church. Their son, Henry, was killed in an accident at the sawmill.

Later, the store was run by Mr. and Mrs. Oliver. They sold groceries, dry goods and hardware to people living in the area.

Ida Geckler, granddaughter of Caleb Plumb, grew up in Plumb's Crossroads and went to school in a cleaned-out granary. Her mother was the teacher and there were six children enrolled in the school. At a rather young age, Ida became the assistant postmaster (regulations were not so strict in those days). She often told of the time a stranger approached the post office window and asked her if she could make out a registered letter for him. She could and promptly did, while the stranger watched her closely. After the letter was stamped and ready for dispatch, the stranger admitted he had been sent by the post office to check out the Plumb Crossing postmaster as they had had a report that she was a small girl and unable to handle the mail.

When supplies were needed for the store, the proprietors would travel to Hamer. There they would take a packet boat down the Miami and Erie Canal to Delphos where they would buy stock for the store and return on the next boat.

Based on an article by Dortha Schaefer in the Paulding County Progress and an article in the Paulding County Republican dated 1949

Charlie and Emma Merriman Porter

Charlie Allen (Al) Porter was born July 30, 1909 to Andrew Alton and Margaret Alice Porter in rural Grover Hill, Jackson Township, Paulding County, Ohio.

Emma Merriman Porter was born March 17, 1919, in Ormus, Noble County, Indiana to Carl Freeman and Edith Lydia Peckhart Merriman. During their courting and early marriage, Charlie and Emma went square dancing at the Wood-U-Drive Inn, roller skating at the Fort Brown Roller Rink, and enjoyed many free shows at Oakwood and Grover Hill. Charlie was the owner of a Harley Davison motorcycle and also had an automobile for courting.

Charlie and Emma were married September 8, 1937 at the United Methodist Church Parsonage in Paulding, Ohio. They have two daughters, Flora Jean Porter Welch and Wilma Marie Porter Fohner. They have five grandchildren and fifteen great-grandchildren.

Emma and Charles Allen Porter

Emma and Charles Allen Porter

Their first home was near Grover Hill, Ohio. A short time after moving there the house was destroyed by fire and everything they had was lost. They moved into Melrose for a short time and then to a house on Fort Brown Road owned by Beechnut Thrasher. Beechnut was a farmer and raised several acres of sweet corn. Beechnut and his wife and Charlie and Emma would work together husking corn for canning. After the Beechnut farm, they moved into Continental. Charlie worked in the Ohio Steel factory in Lima, Ohio for a couple of years, riding to work with Yip Forney. During the 1930's when work was hard to find, Charlie and many other young men worked for the WPA. They were paid $30.00 a month.

The next move was to Beryl Leatherman's property located on Route 66 south of Oakwood. They live there approximately two and a half years.

In 1946 Charlie and Emma purchased 40 acres two miles south of Melrose on Road 177, near the Dan Davison Bridge. It was here that they built their first house. They bought an old house and used the lumber from it along with new lumber to construct the house. They lived there for sixteen years. In 1962 they purchased another 40 acres and built another house on Road 177, one and a half miles south of Melrose. Emma continues to live there today.

Charlie did farming while working at different factories. In 1942 at the beginning of World War II, he began working at Grizzly Manufacturing, Inc. in Paulding, Ohio. He retired from there in 1974. He was a faithful member of the Melrose Community Club, a place where neighbors would meet to have parties. The men would meet there on Sunday afternoons to play cards.

Emma worked at the tomato factory in Paulding, Ohio and Grizzly. While she worked away from home she also cared for her garden and canned many vegetables and fruits. In 1958 Emma attended the Ft. Wayne Beauty College where she obtained her Beauty Salon license. Subsequently she opened her own shop that was built by Charlie.

Emma and Charles Allen Porter   Emma's 90th birthday with Wilma and Flora Jean

Each year the Melrose Elementary School would have a Farmers Institute. A poster contest was held for the children, farmers would bring in their corn and soybeans stalks, and the ladies would bring canned goods. All the items would be judged with a prize going to the best in each category. On Saturday evening there would be a play put on by the people of the community. Emma participated in the plays.

A tradition for many years has been Mom's homemade potato salad and homemade butterscotch pies made from scratch for our family gatherings, where they are enjoyed by all.

Charlie died July 2, 1975 at the age of 66. He is buried at the Little Auglaize Cemetery, Melrose, Ohio.

Emma continued to go to dances until the age of 90. She did do some round dancing in October of this year, 2013. Now on Monday, Tuesday and Thursdays she goes to music played by local musicians.

Submitted by Flora Jean Welch and Wilma Marie Fohner

Mabel and Dorn Porter

Mabel Porter 1913- 1996   Dorn Porter 1910 - 1988

Mabel was the daughter of William and Zoda Greene. Dorn was born in Paulding, the son of Clyde and Anna Porter. Mabel and Dorn Porter were married in 1946. Dorn worked at Grizzly in Paulding. They lived their lives a mile and half from Oakwood. The 40 acre farm ground where Mabel was born was deeded to her Great-Grandfather in 1852. It is still owned by Mabel and Dorn's daughter, Elayne and her husband. Mabel's sisters were Juanita (Greene) Wolfe, Pearl VanCise, Reva and Dorothy Greene.

Submitted by Elayne Porter Mohr

Postmasters

These are the postmasters who have served the Oakwood community:

Name	Date Appointed
George W. Clemens	May 23, 1867
Nathan Whiting	July 26, 1869
Caroline H. Whiting	January 31, 1876
Allen N. Wisely	June 5, 1879
Levi C. Keck	December 24, 1880
George F. Morgan	December 3, 1884
Andrew J. Taylor	October 4, 1888
Ignatius L. Ackley	June 25, 1889
Ohio State Ritchie	May 27, 1893
Dennis Cudhea	February 28, 1898
Harry K. Prentice	September 26, 1910
Edwin M. Stover	March 23, 1922
John M. Harmon	January 7, 1932
Ansel C. Bidlack	February 1, 1936
Dillon W. Staas, Jr.	September 27, 1975
Delores G. (Dearth) Smith	March 17, 1984
Joseph C. Snyder	May 16, 1991
Margaret M. Hastings	June 30, 2012

At one time, being postmaster was a political appointment. Often the location of the post office changed when a new postmaster was appointed. Many of times, the post office was located in a business place that the postmaster operated.

Eventually the post office was located on the northwest corner of West Harmon and First Streets. It remained there for many years until the present building was constructed south of the school in 1960.

For over 100 years, the postmaster was someone who lived in the community. But that changed when the post office appointed someone from among their employees. Dillion Staas was the first non-local postmaster. He lived in Lima, Ohio and commuted to work. Joe Snyder was from Leipsic and Margaret Hastings from Defiance.

Logan Randolph

I remember Logan Randolph as one of the fine citizens of our community along with his wife Mildred. He was an artist at putting paint on walls as well as on canvas. In later life, he and Mildred would walk from their house to downtown Oakwood, he, with one arm thru' Mildred's and the other arm holding a cane, even tho' the cane never touched the sidewalk.

Submitted by Evalena Sharp Fitzwater

The Checker Player

Now there was a checker-playing man! Our own post-master! His name was Mr. Reams. He was a very kindly, calm man. I don't ever remember any time he seemed angry or grouchy. As I remember, he was of average height and weight and had grey hair. He really liked to play checkers. The post office, at that time, was in a building at the corner of 66 and Harmon Street. The checkerboard was set up in the northwest corner of the post office. As I remember, he had a board set-up somewhere else so the interested "checker people" could see what move his partner had made. For, you see, Mr. Reams played checkers by mail. People would come in to see what move Mr. Reams had made or the move his opponent had made and who was winning at the time. Sometimes it would take several months to play a game – maybe even a year. Mr. Reams was a kindly man, a good postmaster and a great checker player.

Submitted by Kathryn Sharp Deatrick

Ohio State Ritchie

Good evening.   Thanks for attending the Oakwood Homecoming Cemetery Walk

My name is Ohio State Ritchie.   I'm known to most as O. S. Ritchie or State. When I became Mayor of Oakwood, I was called "Bender."   I lived over 150 years ago – from 1859, one year before the Civil War broke out until my death in 1939 as the Second World War was starting.

My parents, Mark and Elizabeth, were farmers near Columbus, Ohio. I was the seventh of 10 children but only four of my siblings survived beyond their fifth birthdays.   I had an interest in law; however college was not in the offering for a son of a farmer. Instead, I worked on my own to obtain a teaching certificate.

In 1881 I married Elsie Wright and for a few years owned a general store with my father-in-law.   In time, Elsie bore me three sons: Gaile (1882), Tom (1883) and Mark (1887).

In 1883, my Father passed away and left the farm to my older brother and me.   We were to run the farm and give our two living sisters settlements of $1,500.   Rather than being a farmer, I found I was more eager to see what was beyond the next field and find a new life for me and my family.   So, I pushed on. I sold my share of the farm to my brother and set out to see what this state called 'Ohio' had to offer a young man named 'Ohio State'.

I had received my teaching certificate in 1888, and in 1890, I moved my family to rural Oakwood where I had found a position as a teacher at the Basswood School. A teacher's income was not quite enough to support a family of five, so in addition to teaching, I kept the books for the local tile mill.

After a few years, I was ready for another challenge and in 1892 I purchased my first purebred Chester White sow - the start of my 'Oakwood Herd.' I found the time spent with these animals was quite rewarding and satisfying – quite different than working with books in the school and mill. In addition, A. N. Wiseley and I raised Poland China swine in partnership – The Sunny Side Herd. I am proud to say that our herds were of the most fashionable and up-to-date strains.

In 1893, I received an appointment to become the Postmaster for Oakwood. I would remain in this post till 1898. This was the start of my life in public office. I built a house on the northwest corner of N. First and N. High Streets in Oakwood and moved my family from Basswood.

I was out of the hog business and looking for additional income, so in 1895, Martin Harmon and I bought a hearse and stock of coffins and went into the undertaking business. - didn't need a license in those days. We had a lady assistant and an office over A. N. Wiseley's Grocery Store on First Street.

In 1897, my dear wife, Elsie, passed at the young age of 36. The doctor said it was God's will. She and two of my sons – Mark and Tom – are buried beside me here in Prairie Chapel Cemetery in unmarked graves. I refused to put my money into tomb stones on these graves as I've seen them used for building foundations. I wasn't going to put my money into stones just for other peoples' use when I am gone. I did plant evergreen trees all around my lot, but they grew to considerable height, and I got so many complaints that I had them taken out.

My youngest son's second grade school teacher was Miss Anna Walters – well known to be quite smart and attractive. I made a point to meet her, and even though she was my junior by 17 years, I soon began to court her. Anna agreed to marry me in May 1898, and, at the age of 22, took over the duties of my wife and mother to my three boys – the oldest 16-years- old. I was still interested in law, and I wanted to get out of Oakwood, so I took a job as a Paulding County Deputy Sheriff, and we moved to Paulding. The following year, I ran for Sheriff but was defeated and this hit me hard.

I wanted no more of Paulding! So in 1899, I moved the family back to the house I still owned in Oakwood. I, then, became a partner with my friend A. N. Wiseley in a general store on First Street. This partnership lasted until 1901. I was also during this time a Notary Public.

In 1900, we were blessed with the birth of our daughter, Doris. We were still living on N. First Street, but I started building a new house on the corner of Auglaize and Celina Streets, just down from Anna's folks. The man I sold my current house to wanted to move in right away. Since a new barn was already in place on Auglaize Street, my family moved into the hayloft until the house was finished. Both of my houses still stand today.

1905 found me buying and selling farms, and making loans for a Fort Wayne real estate firm. I was first elected Mayor of Oakwood in 1914 which was quite an honor as I was a Democrat in a mostly Republican town. I was also elected Justice of the Peace for Oakwood in 1915. In 1917, at the onset of World War I, I resigned as Mayor as I got a political appointment as a Capitol Policeman in Washington, DC. My wife and daughter did not move to Washington with me but did visit for two weeks in August 1918. It was an exciting time to be in the Nation's Capital, but I was happy to return to Oakwood in September 1919.

In 1926, I was appointed Mayor of Oakwood when the elected Mayor moved out of town. I won elections for two year terms as Mayor in 1927, 1931 and 1933. I was called upon to marry couples, and to help those in need of paralegal help. In my later years, I wrote land abstracts, was Deputy Registrar and remained a Notary Public.

I lost two of my sons too early in their lives – Mark at the age of 27 from spinal meningitis and Tom at 40 from tuberculosis. Only Tom had married but had no children. My dear wife, Anna, died in a Ft. Wayne hospital in December 1936 while I was serving as Mayor of Oakwood.

My daughter, Doris married Alvin Maddock, and, much to my delight, they had three daughters - Barbra (McCullough), Helen and Iris (Essex). Whenever they came to visit, Iris declared she would cry if I didn't give her a penny. Of course, I was happy to comply so I could watch her rush up to Fruchey's Store to spend it on candy. Yes, it those days there was a large selection of candy to be had for a penny.

In my last years I enjoyed my rocking chair, my pipe and games of solitaire. On April 11, 1939, I suffered a heart attack, but I had little faith

Ben Essex portraying Ohio State Ritchie

in doctors so Doc Burson wasn't called. I felt pretty good the next day, but I knew my time was up and died that afternoon.

I see there is a stone on my grave, probably put here by my daughter, Doris. The U.S. Government must have put a stone on son Gaile's grave for his service in World War I, and next, I see a stone for Tom's wife, Alice. I guess it's OK today as people don't seem to steal tombstone for building foundations.

As portrayed by Great, Great Grandson Ben Essex
Cemetery walk 9/8/2013

Donna Specht Roughton remembers:

I helped my Dad, George Specht, farm when I was in school. One year he gave me a wagon load of beans to sell and I got $400.00 for the load. I thought I was really rich!

In the early 1930's, my Mom, Ethel Specht, entered me in a contest the Oakwood Home Bakery put on. I was 2 years old. The winner was to

Donna's name and picture were featured on the wrapper of the locally baked bread.

have their name and picture on the bread wrapper which was made from wax paper at that time. I won the most votes. I still have 4 of the wrappers. Also have several clippings of the ads that were in the Oakwood News.

My Grandma, Elsie Carnahan, and my Mom, Ethel, worked at the Tomato Factory in the summer. One morning Elsie dressed in the dark. When they got to work, she noticed that she had her dress on wrong side out.

Grandma Elsie would have her grandkids get together on Memorial Day. She would give each of us a flower and we would walk down to the Auglaize River and throw them in the water in remembrance of the service men. She and Grandpa Marion lived in a house across from the Oakwood School. If we grandkids were at her house and there was a thunderstorm, we all had to get up on the feather tick so the lightning would not get us!

My Grandma Amelia Specht, lived in a little house across the lane from ours. An old lady, Artie Williams, lived down west a ways. She was afraid to stay in her house at night. She would walk up to Grandma's house to spend the night, then walk back home in the morning. She was hard of hearing but she could tell you what was said on the telephone party line.

I had a pet pig named Grunter. My sister Apache was in the baby buggy when she was small and the pig rooted the baby buggy over. (She wasn't hurt, just scared.)

This is the story my folks told me: When I was very small we were in a grocery store and Nan Caskey, the undertaker's wife offered me a drink out of her milk bottle. They said I drank all the cream that had settled on top.

When my husband, Todd Roughton, was a telegrapher on the Nickel Plate Railroad, we had a train pass. At that time there were passenger trains running. We would catch one, go up to Cleveland and go to see the Indians play baseball. He was drafted into the Army in 1951. He had his Basic in Camp Gordon, Ga. I went down when he started radio school. We lived there until he was through school. He was sent to Japan and when they learned he was a telegrapher on the railroad, they switched him to the Signal Corps and sent him to Korea. While in Japan, he sent home a 12 piece setting of Noritake China. He also sent a black and silver dress he had made for me (which no longer fits!) but I still have it.

There was a Roller Skating Rink in Fort Brown in the 1930's and 40's. A lot of good times were had there.

The side roads were all stone and were very dusty. In the summer there was oil put on in front of all the houses to keep the dust down.

As a child, I slept on a straw tick. Each year when the thrashing circle would come, they would refill my straw tick with new straw. They always used oat straw rather than wheat straw because oat straw was softer.

When the river froze over in the winter we would go back and clear the snow off and have a game of Hockey. Sometimes we would pull each other on a sled for a while. There was a hill in our woods that was good for sledding. You would go a long ways before you stopped. People would come on Sunday afternoon and have a good time.

The Oakwood School   Tearing down the Oakwood School

It was a sad day in 2003 when they started to demolish the old Oakwood School Building. Twenty-six of us graduated in 1946. Thirteen girls and thirteen boys. Twelve of us went through all twelve grades together. They were: Phyllis Kohart, Virginia Mead, Marilyn Keck, Shirley Carnahan, Paul Burson, Norman McClure, John Mark Hill, Darrel Sherman, Archie Grimes and myself. My mother, Ethel, graduated in 1926. She started in a one room school called Basswood, north of Oakwood. She came to Oakwood in the 4th grade. She told me about her and a brother going to Basswood in a horse and buggy. The horse would go back home by himself.

There was a big train wreck in Oakwood in April of 1956. Todd and I lived next to the United Brethren Church. We heard a loud noise that woke us up. We looked out and could see that it was foggy. A little later someone called us and said the train had wrecked. What we thought was fog was really dust! There were sides of beef in a car or two, cars of oranges, soup, plus many more things. The soup cans lost the labels. We had surprise soup many meals. At that time, Todd and J. L. Treece had a photography business as a hobby. The railroad officials wanted pictures taken of the wreck. Both Todd and J. L. were at work so I took the big camera over and took the pictures that they wanted.

Train wreck

In 1995, my sister, Apache, said we should get a picture of at least one barn in Ohio's 88 counties. We already had many pictures of barns in Paulding County. As you know big old barns are a thing of the past. We spent many weekends traveling in Ohio taking Barn pictures. Apache's husband was our driver. In 1998 they started to paint The Bicentennial Logo on one barn in each county. Scott Hayan from Belmont County was the painter. The first barn painted was in Belmont County. The last one painted was in Sandusky County in 2002. Apache and I made the trip there to watch it being done. Paulding County was #40. We went to see it painted also. We have several books of barn pictures. Of course we took more than one in each county. A lot of the barns we have pictures of are now gone. Even some that had the Bicentennial Logo on. One weekend we traveled 1200 miles and never got out of Ohio.

A bicentennial barn

Paulding County's barn

State Route 66 over Auglaize River in Oakwood has had three bridges I can remember. Don't know when the first one was built. It was a narrow steel bridge. In 1950 a new wider steel bridge was built. The old bridge was moved to one side, with a temporary road made over it to be used while the new bridge was built. It even had lights on top of it for a while. In October 1992 that bridge was torn down. A new cement one was built. It took 2 dynamite blasts to get the middle span down. The first blast just dented the steel a little. To get to the other side of the river you had to either go to the County Line Bridge or the Charloe Bridge. Both ways were a long way around.

The old bridge comes down!

S and S Locker Plant

In 1951 our parents Harold and Bonnie Shisler moved back to their home town of Oakwood, Ohio. They had previously lived for 10 years in Detroit, Michigan. They returned to manage and run the S&S Locker plant and grocery store. In the 50's and 60's locker plants were popular as people didn't have freezers. At the S&S people could rent a locker which was a small box in a large freezer like room. They were given a key and could come when they wanted and put meat etc. in their locker. Our dad would butcher and cut up their beef or hog if they wanted and put it in their locker.

There were many interesting things that happened at the S&S, but one that stands out in our minds was the time that Aunt Jemima came to visit. I imagine that the Aunt Jemima Pancake Company had suggested to our parents that having an Aunt Jemima Day would get people to come to the store for this special occasion. The lady that portrayed Aunt Jemima came from Toledo dressed as an ordinary person, but she brought a suitcase that carried her Aunt Jemima clothes. She went to the restroom and came out as Aunt Jemima. She spent the day making and serving pancakes and promoting Aunt Jemima pancake mix. My sister and I were very excited when we got our picture taken with her. It was a day we will always remember.

Janis Shisler Lentz, Aunt Jemina, Susann Shisler Williams

Free shows were a great adventure when we were young and living in the small town of Oakwood, Ohio. Every Saturday night and sometimes on Wednesday free shows were shown where the Oakwood Park is now located on a large screen that was probably made from an old white sheet. People would come as it was getting dusk and bring blankets and chairs and settle in for a night of movies. Hut Doster and his boys brought the projector and ran the movies out of the back of their truck. There was a cartoon and the movies were mostly westerns. There was an intermission and people went to one of the stores close by or the popcorn stand that was run by our two aunts Zylpha Shisler and Pauline Shisler. Zylpha was our dad's brother Delbert's wife. Delbert ran a mink farm out near the county line. Pauline's husband was our dad's brother Lester's wife. Lester sold cars and had a garage. The different businesses paid a small fee for the movies as it was thought to bring people to town and then they would shop. The free shows went on even if it rained unless it was a downpour. There is something about sitting on a blanket under the stars with family and friends that is hard to forget.

Railroads have always been an important part of small towns like Oakwood. It brought the mail and it provided a mode of transportation for the small towns. In 1910 the railroad was the way our grandparents, Newton and Ida Hays, arrived in the small community of Oakwood. They had come to Oakwood from Seymore, Illinois, because they had bought farm land northeast of Oakwood. They had loaded all their belongings on the train in Illinois and traveled east to Ohio. When they arrived in Oakwood they unloaded their wagons and horses and cattle and drove out to their new home in Ohio. In 1928 when our grandfather got sick he was taken to Fort Wayne, Indiana, for surgery. He passed away in the hospital and was brought back to his home town of

Oakwood on the train, our grandmother traveling with his body. In 1962, when my grandmother's sister in Illinois died, she went to the Oakwood Depot and talked to L. E. Speakman, the depot agent, about getting a ticket to Seymore, Illinois. Grandmother and I got on the train in Oakwood and traveled to Illinois for the funeral. Riding the train was nothing new for me as I had gone on the train to Fort Wayne, Indiana with my mother and sister for a shopping trip while we were in our teens. Our senior class the class of 1961 left from the Oakwood Depot on a sunny Sunday afternoon for Washington D. C. Parents and friends came to see us off and we returned the same way.

Submitted by Janis Lentz & Suzann Williams

School Days

Back in the late 30's and early 40's it was the practice of the students of the Commercial Department of our school to publish a monthly mimeographed paper called the "Green Lite" which was sold to the student body for five cents a copy. It recorded the activities and interests of the school in typical high school prose, and the following articles were taken from this paper.

A few will recall perhaps not many more, that our athletic teams were originally known as the "Green Devils", which was a good fightin' name but presented somewhat of a problem in good taste, especially when the varsity and reserve squads were designated as the "Big Devils" and the "Little Devils". The powers that be decided that a change was in order, and the following article was written relative to that change. It appeared in the October issue of the "Green Lite" in 1941. The title of the article was "BOBCATS!"

"Let's all hail the brand new name of our fightin' forces, the BOBCATS! I'm sure we all agree that it's a swell name, which is only fittin' for a swell bunch of guys and gals who will carry the banner far for a swell school, Oakwood Hi.

At least we feel when we are giving a rousing cheer for the old Alma Mater we aren't getting a wee bit on the profane side. I think we should all get behind the teams, whether it be in baseball, basketball or intra-murals sports and show the old fighting spirit and sportsmanship our school is noted for."

Anonymous contribution to Oakwood News

Oakwood School, fall of 1900 to the spring 1902

The school was a four room brick with box stoves as heating equipment and wood for fuel. Only three rooms were in use as this time.

Teachers for the first year were: primary, Mrs. L. M. Eschbach; intermediate, Miss Jessie Beaman; upper grades and high school, L. M Eschbach. For the second year they were: primary, Mrs. Emma Hakes; intermediate, Mrs. L. M. Eschbach and L. M. Eschbach for the upper grades and high school. Frank Hakes was the janitor. During the later part of January 1901, Miss Beaman became ill and I substituted for her for one week. No graduates in 1901. The senior class of 1902 consisted of Irvin and Reuben Lighthill, Tom Hall Ritchie, Fred Petteford, Essa Harmon, Zella Wiseley and myself.

The following is a partial list of the other pupils in Mr. Eschbach's room that year: Ray Welty, Robert C. Christy, William Funk, Lillian Myers, Bessie Rhees, Mary Bidlack, Ina Whiting, Dessie Bush and Eathel Fuller.

The Commencement of 1902 was held in the M. E. Church with a full house attending. The program consisted of an oration or some other number by each member of the class, a piano duet by Miss Lulu Hakes and I. Miss Hakes was the pianist for the evening. The class address was given by the Hon. O. T. Corson, Supt. of the Department of

Education, State of Ohio. Members of the Board of Education were: S. S. Shisler, M. W. Harmon and R. M. Weible.

W. V. Kretzinger

Writing in the Oakwood News 1955

School Days

As I think back to my school days and think how some of the things have changed, for instance I walked three quarters of a mile to a country school known as the "Fitzwater School". Then when I entered high school at Oakwood I still had to walk three quarters of a mile to get a ride, no, not on a school bus but with Louise (Bauer) Stover and Inez Weible. The only bus at that time was the one from Melrose.

Melrose School Bus

Another thing, we had to purchase our own books. Harmon's Drug store was a mighty busy place at the beginning of the year. Or if you were fortunate you could purchase some used ones from other students the price depending upon what condition the book was in. I will say some were well used or should I say poorly used? By the end of the first month, most all the students would have their books purchased.

We also had a graduation exercise when we left the eighth grade and entered into high school. I remember the girls wore black pleated skirts and white middie blouse with a large black bow at the neckline. I recall my father and I going to this affair in a buggy, however, before I was out of high school, we had purchased a new Ford, and if I remember correctly, it cost a little over $400. Side curtains and all.

The first few weeks in high school we got acquainted. Those of us from the country were rather backward. We didn't come and go and mingle with so many people like the students from the country do now. I am sure that most people could tell the country students but by graduation time most students had lost their backwards ways and many graduated with honors.

These might be some of the changes since my school days but the fundamental things that were taught then remain the same today. A reputation can be made in an hour but character is what you are through the years. I would like to mention a few of the teachers who helped 22 pupils to graduate in the class of 1928: J. M. Reed, Supt.; R. C. Niswander, principal and supt.; Miss Enid Funk; Florence Thrasher; Majorie Dunipace; Clara Belle Stump, music; Lester Hurley; Loyal Burkholder; Fern Kimmel; P. D. Koeppe; Annie Ritchie, home ec.; and Vivian Murdock, music.

Doris Grimes Adams

Writing in the Oakwood News in 1955

My School Days at Oakwood Hi

My school days began in September of 1919. I attended the Lighthill School which was located two miles north and a mile east of town. The teacher was E. J. Kretzinger. The next fall I was back at the same school with the same teacher. But after a month or six weeks of school, we were transferred to Oakwood. That ended the good old days at Lighthill School.

In coming to school here in town, Miss Bernice Grube was my teacher. It was then I became acquainted with Harley Shisler, Anita Speakman, and a few others that belonged to the class of '31. We were classmates from the 2nd grade on thru the 12th. Our third grade teacher was Miss Faye Neds. During this term our room put on the program at one of the PTA meetings. We presented the short play of "Little Red Riding Hood". I don't remember all of the characters but Harley played the role of the Big Bad Wolf. Marie Fogle was Little Red Riding Hood and I was the grandmother.

Our 4th grade teacher was Mrs. Anna Ritchie, who is well remembered by many from the community. Miss Lillian Gieger from Bluffton was our 5th grade teacher. For our 6th grade teacher, the majority of us had Miss Jenny Gray, who is also well remembered by many Oakwoodites. A few of the 6th graders were down in Mr. Schooley's room. The next year, which was 1925, Jr. Hi was started. We 7th graders had two teachers, E. J. Kretzinger and Mrs. Anna Ritchie. To help us thru the 8th grade, we were fortunate in again having the same two teachers. We also had three of the high school instructors: Miss Florence Thrasher, Miss Fern Kimmel and Lyle Burkholder.

In September, 1927, we were the freshmen class. Mr. Burkholder was our class advisor. Mabel Bidlack was president and Helen Kretzinger was secretary and treasurer. At the beginning of the 2nd semester, we faced a great sorrow. Our classmate, Helen, left us to join the Great Master of all. At the close of this term of school, R. C. Niswander left Oakwood. I believe this was also Mrs. Ritchie's last year of teaching.

The following fall we were back as sophomores. Mr. Koeppe was superintendent, and Miss Maude Chase was the new Latin and Home Ec. teacher. Miss Kimmell was our class advisor. Hilda Wurm was pres., and Clarence Bauer, sec.-treas. The class held a party at the home of Avis Boyd during this year. Homemade ice cream and cake was enjoyed by everyone present. At the close of this school year, Mr. Burkholder who had been the math teacher and football coach for the past 3 years, left OHS.

In the fall of '29 we were Juniors. We again chose Miss Kimmell as our class advisor. Madeline Parrish was president and Marie Fogle sec.-treas. Ira Benedict and E. J. Kretzinger were added to the list of high school teachers this year. Mr. Benedict took Mr. Burkholder's place as football coach. Under the direction of Mr. Koeppe we presented our class play, "The Empty House", in the spring of that year. At the close of this school year, Mr. Koeppe and Mr. Benedict left OHS.

The fall of '30, we were Seniors. Mr. Codding was the new superintendent. Miss Watkins was the music teacher. Ralph Blauvelt, the math teacher and football coach. The remaining list of teachers was the same as before: Miss Kimmell, Miss Chase and Mr. Kretzinger. In October of this year, some of us enjoyed the trip to Springfield, O., attending the George Roger Clark Sesquicentennial.

Just before Christmas we received our class rings. On February 4th, we held a class party in the new gym. This year was the first that Oakwood played basketball.

Our farewell class party was held at the home of Clarence Bauer. We graduated in May, 1931. This ended our school days at Oakwood Hi. We were the first class to graduate in the new auditorium and we were proud of it.

Wilhelmina Moore, Class of 1931
Writing in the Oakwood News

My Days at O. H. S.

When I became a student of Oakwood High School in 1926, it was the proverbial small high school without a gymnasium, it did have the "old auditorium" which was gradually converted into classrooms.

Our superintendent was R. C. Niswander with other members of the staff: Lyle Burkholder, Lester Hurley, Maude Chase, E. J. Kretzinger, Anna Ritchie and Miss Thrasher. High school at this time was largely textbook study. There was meager educational equipment available, altho' we did have reasonably new "manual training" equipment.

Our visual aids consisted of a few maps and, as I recall, one microscope. Physical Education classes were held outside when weather permitted. Our history class was held in the auditorium. This was the period of silent movies and the first talking pictures – the vita-phone.

Football and baseball were the major sports. School plays, the annual Farmers Institutes, school operettas were big events. Lindbergh became famous. The first "Oakleaf" was printed in 1929.

The front sidewalk was built by the class of 1929 and well I remember the ceremony at which time Charles Stanton's Latin book as well as many other items of "historical lore" were sunk in the cement sidewalk (in a southeast corner of one block).

Rill Weible, Class of 1930

Writing for the Oakwood News

School memories

While cleaning house the other day, I came across my copy of the 1938 Oakleaf. Immediately, housework was forgotten and I sat down to leaf thru its pages. As I turned each page I turned back the years and was living again that most wonderful time of a person's life, their Senior year in high school. Having joined the class in my Junior year I don't know much of what happened in the ten years before but those last two years at Oakwood Hi held many wonderful memories for me.

Our class was composed of 15 boys and 15 girls which was rather unusual we thought. Of these thirty people, twenty-eight are still living.

G. L. Rader was superintendent at the time and E. J. Kretzinger, principal. We selected Rachel Pierce as our class sponsor and Raymond Ice was our class president. Under their leadership we set our goal on something that had never been done before in Oakwood Hi, we planned a three-day trip to Niagara Falls. We worked hard, planned a "Here 'Tis" Carnival, sponsored skating parties, held bake sales, even made homemade ice cream and sold it. We went over the top, chartered a bus and spent three, fun-filled days at Niagara Falls, chaperoned by Miss Pierce and Mr. Asmus.

This was the year that the present Alma Mater was written in a music appreciation class under Miss Pierce. This year, also, we robed the Girl's Glee Club for the first time. Their Christmas and Easter concerts were very impressive as they slowly filed down the aisles of the Methodist Church, each carrying a lighted candle and singing, "O, Come All Ye Faithful."

In 1937, the combined Glee clubs presented, "The Gypsy Rover", with Paul Shisler and Leona Matson singing the leads; and in 1938, Leona and Harold Grosenbacher sang the leading roles in "Jerry of Jericho Road". Do you remember how Miss Pierce went around for days afterwards asking if she had thanked us for her gardenias? Also, in 1937, Oakwood's first school band was organized under the direction of Mr. Glen Sickafus. Thelma Wolff was chosen drum majorette and how proud we were to see her picture in the Ft. Wayne paper the day after the Peony Festival Parade in Van Wert.

The Girl's Sextette entered the state competition that year with their arrangement of "Gute Nacht." These girls were: Leona Matson, Minnie Cunningham, Lenore Matson, Janice Rickner, Alvada Weible and Ruth Dotterer.

In our Junior year, we decided to revive the old tradition of Flunk Day and on a beautiful spring day about a week before school was out several car loads of Juniors headed north. We went as far as Jackson, Michigan before we turned around. We took our punishment like ladies and gentlemen but talked about the escapade for weeks afterwards – except in the presence of Mr. Asmus who ignored the whole thing as tho' it had never happened.

On March 22, 1938, the Senior class appeared at school in short dresses and knee pants, complete with suckers, apples and bubblegum, for their annual Kid Day. The affair was climaxed by a party in the school gym that evening.

Finally came the last week, the goal toward which we had been striving for twelve years. Rev. Fremont McCague delivered the Baccalaureate sermon in the school auditorium on Sunday evening, May 22. The on Friday evening, following an address by Mr. D.H. Sutton of Ohio State University, Mr. Rader handed each of us our diploma.

Claudine Burt Thompson
Writing in the Oakwood News

The school that most of us remember was built in 1918 after the previous school on that site was torn down. That school was three stories and on the top story was an assembly room which was later subdivided into class rooms.

In 1931 a gymnasium/auditorium was added to the back of the building. It had a stage and a playing floor. With that addition, the school was able to have a basketball team.

By the late 1940's the school was badly overcrowded. In August 1951, construction was started on an addition which was ready to use in the fall of 1952. This addition to the south of the original building had 3 elementary class rooms, a band room, a vocational agriculture room, two locker rooms with showers, and a 100 seat cafeteria. It also included administrative offices. The construction of this building cost $145,000 plus $15,000 for furnishings and equipment. There were over 400 students enrolled at that time.

A further addition was added in 1957. This addition to the east housed several elementary classrooms plus home-economics rooms and a new science lab.

Faye Leatherman Sharp

My memory is of my grandmother, Sydney "Faye" Sharp. She was a very giving person.

Faye Sharp

As a child, I remember getting to go to the attic, going on an adventure every little girl loves, looking through old trunks and playing dress up. In the attic you were in a different time. Every shelf or corner had a unique treasure; I don't think grandma ever threw anything away! She had the walls papered with all different pictures from old calendars and flowers, she loved flowers. Dahlias especially, she was known for her garden full of them.

I don't know how she did it in the tiny space she had for a kitchen, but every time you went to her house, she would fix a wonderful meal, even if you just popped in she would manage to make a feast. Her homemade mush would be my favorite; she also made the best molasses cookies!

Grandma was devoted to God and her family. We had many wonderful times with her. She was an honored citizen of the Oakwood Homecoming in 1980. I still have her plaque displayed in my room.

Submitted by Sherry Sharp Schilt

Faye Sharp

To a woman of great intelligence, beauty, patience and creativity –

Her hands did touch the soil and make great beauty grow

Did touch the palette of the rainbow and made the colors, blend, just so-

Did touch a piece of cloth and make a fashion thus –

Reading was a "must" with her – God's word and "minds" both old and new!

Traveling was a special joy – the Smokies, Florida, Las Vegas, Wisconsin, Pike's Peak!

Beautiful, Gentle, Calm, Steadfast

A life filled with tragedies, some great – some small.

A life filled with joys, some great – some small.

Given strength by God on many days,

Blest by God in many ways.

-In praise of and with love to my mother – Sidney Faye Leatherman Sharp

Submitted by Kathryn Sharp Deatrick

LuAnn Sharp remembers:

These are some of the many things I remember about living in Oakwood:

My brother, Ned Sharp and his friend Dick Stover, while going to high school, would run trap lines in an attempt to trap muskrats along the Auglaize River. They would get up early in the morning to do this before going to school. One very cold December morning they did their usual routine of going out in the boat to the site of their traps, tying up the boat, and attending to the traps. As luck would have it, when they turned around to get back in the boat, it wasn't there. Somehow it had come untied and had drifted out in the middle of the river. They had no other recourse but to get the boat in order to get back to go to school. My brother took off all his clothes, jumped in the river and swam for the boat. I remember him saying he swam through pieces of ice. He was a good swimmer and brought the boat back. The thing that saved him was the long-legged wool underwear of our grandfather (Dr. Frank Leatherman) that he was wearing, which kept him very warm when he put them back on under his outer clothes. This didn't stop them from continuing to run their trap lines.

While in elementary school, Judy Spencer and I would run off to what was then called Dead Man's Road (now called Chapel Lane), and pick wild strawberries that grew along the side of the road. This was called Dead Man's Road because there was and still is a cemetery at both ends of the road.

I say "ran off" because I would not tell my mother (Faye Sharp) where I was going for fear she would not let me go. Needless to say, when I returned home, I was met with my mother holding a paddle and chasing me all the way from the barn to the house. I wonder why this never kept me from doing it all again. Those berries were so sweet!

The Auglaize River provided a lot of entertainment for the residents of Oakwood--- swimming, boating, fishing. For me it was fishing. As a little girl of 10 years of age, I would get one of my grandfather's cane fishing poles, find some night crawlers, put them in a little container, get a bucket and head for the river. Yes, I could actually put one of those squirming worms on the fishhook. One particular day I crossed the bridge, which was an entirely different bridge than the one that is there now, and went to the other side of the river. Just by a stroke of luck, I found a good fishing hole and every time I threw my line in I would bring up a bluegill. You can imagine how happy that made me. That day I carried home many fish in my bucket.

My brothers, Ned and Harry Sharp, took me snipe hunting one day along with some other friends of theirs, when I was only about six years old. They convinced me that I would be holding a bag and they would shoo the bird into it. They took me down to the street that goes along the side of where Gerald Shisler lived and on back to a field along the river. I remember I could feel the stubbles in the field on the bottom of my bare feet. They, of course, had me turn around, telling me I had to be very quiet. I kept waiting and waiting. When finally nothing happened, I turned around and everyone was gone. I'm sure they all could hardly contain their laughter until they were out of earshot. I walked home alone and I don't know if my mother ever found out or not. Probably not, because I don't think my brothers ever got punished for that.

LuAnn Sharp
Indianapolis

Lizzie Shisler

The modern saying is: "That good neighbors keep good fences". My mother, Mrs. Lizzie Shisler, who died December 20th, 1944 said: "That good neighbors need no fences."

In our family there were five boys and two girls, in which my mother shared everything alike. My mother did not go very far in school, nor did she have a master's degree in books. Her masterpiece was her family and watching them grow. She did not mind the washing, cooking and getting up nights with the babies but her worry was teaching us how to live and work together in a community as a whole. I have heard her say, "I would not give a million dollars for any one of the seven nor would I give a dollar for another one." She did not spend her time and one half of her money in a beauty shop or at a ten cent show but her time was spent with her family, cooking, sewing, and making clothes so all could go to school...she said there were three things you all can do if you are poor: be honest, be clean and learn to share with each other.

Her beauty came from within and not from powder and paint as a lot of modern mothers worry about now days. She taught us how to be thankful for the small things in life and the big will come later as you work for them. The interest I have in human relations comes to me naturally as it was taught to us when we were small in the home.

The Shisler Brothers:
Rear: Harley, Harold, Lester Front: Paul and Delbert

When I was small, neighborhoods were true communities, bound by common interest in each other's families. The joy and sorrow of each family was shared by all. My mother was a friend of all people regardless of the difference of religious belief or color. Our home had a warm welcome at all times for everyone. When we got ready to eat if anyone was there they were the same as one of the family. We borrowed from the neighbors but she taught us to pay back with gospel measure and be honest to all. We had to help the old or the sick and be kind to everyone we knew.

My mother's life was a fine example of true Christianity in action and not in words. Her life was a shining example for any mother to pattern after. Her friends were from all walks of life. She said: "No one is too low but what you can help to lift them up, nor no one too high but what the Lord can bring them down to everyday living."

None of we seven children have reached her measure in a living brotherhood, however, each one of us, I am certain, has inherited some share of her interest in building a better community to live in.

Harley Shisler

Writing in the Oakwood News

Lizzie Shisler

I'd like to talk a little bit about our neighbor. She was known to us as Lizzie – Lizzie Shisler. She lived across the alley from us – on the corner of Harmon and River Streets. Our side door was across the alley from her back door. At the time I knew her she had a "bunch of boys". They were in high school during my grade school years and were on the football team – yes, Oakwood at one time had a football team.

As little girls, my sister and I were outside a lot and got scrapes and bruises as well as getting burns and hurt from playing and working inside. Whenever we got burned or got a scrape or cut, we would run across the alley to Lizzie to have her "blow" away the hurt. She always would do that and we were happy again. She must have "put up" with a bunch of stuff from having an all-male household. At times, when I was probably five or six the Shisler boys had a bunch of milk goats. The goats were tied in the yard and were milked every day. Since I seemed to be "sickly", it was determined that the goat milk would be good for me so I drank goat milk every day.

I'll always remember Lizzie with kindly thoughts and for her ability to "blow away" the hurt from scrapes and especially the hurt of burns.

Submitted by Kathryn Sharp Deatrick

The Schick – Stephens family

Precious memories of growing up in Oakwood shared by the grown children of Gilbert and Colleen Schick: Gloria, Ruthann, Bobby, and Lesa.   By Gloria (Schick) Grimes

Our dad Gilbert's grandmother, Lucinda Stephens, was born July 8, 1870 and died June 12, 1966. She was a great inspiration to all of us. Our great grandmother was a wonderful cheerful lady and we were blessed have our Great Grandmother, that the entire family loving called "Mommie", until she was nearly 96 years old. Mommie lived right across from the Oakwood School and we spent many afternoons after band practice stopping by and visiting her. Holidays were spent at her house with an array of bountiful foods that the family would bring to share with our grandparents, Arthur and Elsie Schick, and cousins of our dad Gilbert's sister Jessie Leatherman's family. Every year we would go to her home for The Oakwood Homecoming. We looked forward to this all day event every Labor Day. The Parade was a highlight as it passed right in front of her house on Route 66. The day was filled with activities with carnival games rides and an art show in yard in front of the school. Her home was a place of wonderful memories where stories of her childhood were often shared. In 1959, Mommie was interviewed for an article in the Oakwood paper and personally shared her memories of that time gone by of the canal boat days. Mrs. Stephens was born in a one room log cabin one and a half miles north of Junction. Her parents were Jacob and Elisabeth Brown. Her father earned his living in buying and making ship timber. The family moved to Blue Creek and later to Charloe where her father Mr. Brown hauled timber through the canal, and floated it from Defiance to Toledo.

Elsie Schick (age 16) and
her mother Lucinda Stephens

Arthur and Elsie Schick

From Charloe the family moved to Paulding where Mrs. Stephens started her first term of school in a one-room building. During that time teachers boarded in the Brown home. After the timber was mostly cut off the family moved to Spencerville, Ohio, and each spring her father Mr. Brown engaged in floating timber on the canal to Toledo, and in the winter hauled the logs by bobsled from the woods. As the years went by, the family moved to a place two and one-fourth miles north of Junction, Ohio, and there Mrs. Stephens recalls that she used to watch the Packet, a canal boat, as it traveled between Defiance and Delphos once a week. Mrs. Stephens remembers that she, at that time, made trips to Defiance from Junction on the canal boat and would return in the afternoon. Mrs. Stephens stayed at home and helped her mother with housework until her twenty-fourth birthday. Then on September 19, 1894 she married Charlie Stephens who died on April 30, 1922. Their grandson, Gilbert Charles Schick, born just two months before on February 28, 1922, was named after his grandfather Charlie Stephens. In 1903 Mr. and Mrs. Stephens bought the Dave Thomas farm on Fort Brown Road. They were the parents to one child Elsie Irene. Mrs. Lucinda Stephens continued to live on the farm after the untimely death of her husband Charlie until October 30, 1935 when she moved to the home located across from the Oakwood School. Our great grandmother Lucinda Stephens lived in and around Oakwood most of her entire life. She attended the Evangelical United Brethren Church for more than fifty years. Mommie loved to read and had extraordinary talent as she handmade beautiful crochet doilies and detailed handmade embroidery items.

Our dad Gilbert's parents, Arthur Washington and Elsie (Stephens) Schick, were married in February 1917. They celebrated over fifty years of marriage, and were the parents of two children, Gilbert and Jessie. Grandpa was born December 16, 1892 and passed away on April 2, 1971. Grandma was born March 6, 1896 and died March 2, 1979. Arthur moved to Ohio from Washington, Illinois in his early twenties and was from the Mennonite Church. When he arrived he lived with his sister Mrs. Aaron (Minnie) Stoller, also a native of Illinois, in Latty, Ohio to work on her family farm. It was during this time that he and our grandmother Elsie Stephens met. They established their first home in Broughton, Ohio before moving to the farm in Oakwood on the Fort Brown road. In the earliest years of their marriage Arthur worked at a wagon terminal in Defiance, Ohio. A few years later they started working the family farm full time. They were both hardworking on the farm. We have many wonderful memories of our grandparents living just across the field from us our entire childhood. We spent many of our days riding bikes down the road and up the long lane to their house. In the evenings they would hold the jump rope for us while we played. A favorite memory is of Grandpa taking all the grandchildren to Humpty Dumpty in Defiance. Grandma was a wonderful hostess. Her table was always fully set and had beautiful linens. The meals were like feasts and always ended with delicious homemade pies. In the summer we enjoyed going to the Independence State Dam and had hand-turned ice cream celebrating our great grandmother's birthday. They were also active members of the local Evangelical United Brethren Church in Oakwood where Grandma used her talent in the kitchen to help.

Our parents, Gilbert Charles and Lois Colleen (Jeffery) Schick, were married November 7, 1948. They celebrated sixty-two years of marriage together. Dad was born February 28, 1922. He shares memories of walking to the Oakwood School with his neighbors. He tells stories of swimming in the Auglaize River and enjoyed one of the most popular activities for teens and young adults from around the area as he often went roller skating at the Fort Brown Skating Rink. Dad has been a hardworking dedicated farmer his entire life. As a child he worked alongside his father on the family farm. He recalls that at the age of just thirteen, plowing the fields with his horses. Mom was born September 19, 1928 and passed away February 21, 2011. She was raised on a farm in Paulding, Ohio, and was the daughter of Leo and Neva (Johnson) Jeffery. Neva was a school teacher in Paulding County as Mom grew up, while her dad worked the family farm. Mom helped her dad in the fields just as she would one day help her future husband. She worked as a secretary at Walley Agricultural Service prior to their marriage.

Gilbert and Colleen Schick

Dad first met Mom by offering to help her with a flat tire. They spent their two week honeymoon driving their 1948 Ford to California via the now historical Route 66. Mom and Dad spent their entire marriage working alongside each other. Mom and Dad worked a lifetime together raising livestock and grain crop farming. We would have Farm Bureau Council meetings with the farm neighbors, and they were members of the Grange in Charloe, Ohio. They enjoyed raising their family, and, as kids, holidays and birthdays were always special for us. Summer family vacations were spent traveling the country to different states and going to the lake. Our parents helped us with our projects as we were members of the "We Mean Business 4-H group", and our mom and Doris Kohart were the advisers. Mom was also a member of the "Everwilling Home Demonstration Club" with many of the women of the Oakwood area. They were active members of the Woodlawn United Methodist Church working with their friends and neighbors in Oakwood. Together they attended Paulding United Methodist the last 20 years, and Dad still attends today. Mom represented the state of Ohio at the American Mothers Association as Mother of the Year in Puerto Rico in the 1980's. Dad was a member of the Defiance Gideon International Camp and Mom served as the President of the Ladies Auxiliary. They were also honored as "Mrs. and Mrs. Oakwood" at Oakwood Homecoming. Gilbert and Colleen have nine grandchildren who were all raised in the Oakwood area just miles from our childhood home. They each have wonderful memories of growing up in the country and spending many days at Grandma and Grandpa Schick's house with their cousins. Mom lived a full life loving her family. Dad will celebrate his ninety-second birthday in 2014 and still lives in our family home on the farm. He spends his days attending church, looking through photos of his family, playing dominoes with visitors, watching his favorite sports and game shows on television, but most of all he enjoys visiting with his family which he has had the pleasure of meeting and knowing what has grown into five generations.

Horace Shriver: This is your life!

Horace B. Shriver was born September 4, 1869 at Royal Oak, in Brown Township.

You are the son of Samuel Shriver. At the age of 86 you still have gardening as your hobby. Early to bed and late to rise, is your recipe for living to an old age. Here as a boy you grew into Manhood with two brothers and three sisters, Virgil, Ossie and George; and Mrs. George Buyyard and Mrs. D. Klinger. You assisted your father in the general store at Royal Oak, which is one of the ghost towns that do not exist anymore. Your father also bought ship timber and timber for the hoop and stave factory. At this time they started to build some of the railroads and a lot of timber was purchased for the railroad, pilings, etc.

You attended the Royal Oak School and your favorite teacher was Tillie Keefer of Charloe. You spent a lot of time hunting, fishing, skating and swimming in the old Miami Erie Canal. You watched the canal boats go by as they were pulled by one to four mules, on each boat, according to the size of the boats. You could go from Royal Oak to Defiance one day, and back the next, and from Royal Oak to Delphos in the same length of time. There were no steam packets allowed on the canal as they tore up the banks too much. The first mule packet line started back in the year of 1850. It was started by Cap Cleason who had his headquarters at Royal Oak. It was also one of the first post offices in Brown Township. Cap Cleason ran the packet line a number of years until his death, then Cap Wise took over. Cap Booth was also another captain who did not like bumped bridges. On one of his trips he got his four mules to run and hit the pole on the bridge so hard that it knocked a hole in his boat and sank a load of salt in the canal. On another occasion at the draw bridge, the man forgot to shut the bridge and 16 railroad cars fell into the canal.

You also helped to get two of Charles Kohart's little sisters out of the canal after they had broken though the ice and drowned. This was on New Year's Day at 10:00 in the morning, 1885. Your first job working out, at the age of 16, was at the hoop and stave factory at Melrose. You received 75 cents a day, and worked from 7 to 7. After the factories closed at Melrose you moved to Oakwood. Then you served in the Spanish-American War until it was over. You "batched it" above Charlie Dickey's building, then owned by Harry Prentice, postmaster and school teacher. Here are a few of the things that I remember about Horace:

He was the most noted fisherman that Oakwood ever had for a number of years, or until "Dan Boone" (Arthur Grindstaff) moved to town. Boone in my estimation now holds the belt. You, Horace, used to catch fish by the wheelbarrow full; your best customers were John Fuller and Frank Harmon. We kids used to sell you light bulbs at one cent each. You put a line and hook on these bulbs and let them float down the river. Every two hours, you would run them. One occasion, as I recall, a big rain and wind came up and you could not find your 125 bulbs. However, after rowing your boat as far as Charloe, you found them in the brush.

Although you had no children, you were always good to us kids, you also had a pet ferret you hunted with. It was tame and would sit on your lap when you fed it. One day while hunting the game warden came upon Horace so he put the ferret in his hip boot, and when the warden searched him, nothing was found. You spent a lot of time working on the railroad, then you started to weigh sugar beets at Oakwood. Lem Reams, now deceased, was the field man. Coal was hard to get for two reasons: one for the lack of money, and the other, for the scarcity of coal, however, when you cleaned out the coal cars you saved all the coal and put it upstairs in your room. Sometimes you sold it or gave it to someone that was old. One time you had so much in your room the ceiling of the post office started to break through.

In the year of 1928, at the age of 59, you married Eva Hakes and moved to Marcellus, Mich. There you have lived for the past 26 years on a small truck farm raising fruits and vegetables. When I told Horace that the WPA tore the old aqueduct down in 1934, it made tears come to his eyes. He said. "I have a lot of pleasant memories about that old place."

Although you live in Michigan, your heart is back in Oakwood. You attend all the homecomings you possibly can. Here is a secret that Horace told me. "The grass is greener, the girls are sweeter and kiss better around Oakwood than any town in the world."

Harley Shisler
Writing for the Oakwood News 1955

Slinging Mud Balls

I spent my childhood years living on a farm just south of Melrose and being a Paulding County boy I knew a lot about clay, which some people called mud. It was great boyhood fun after a rain or rainy season to find a good lump of clay, got to the apple tree in the back yard and cut a good long, straight but slightly flexible stick about three feet long (the ones dad called "suckers") and then look out, I was ready to sling some mud. I would make clay "Mud" balls about the size of a small chicken egg or a little smaller than a golf ball and put the mud ball on the end of the apple stick. Then with a mighty heave of a long overhead or sidearm arc, I would whip the stick around and the mud ball would come flying off the end of the stick as it headed for outer space over the top of the barn. I learned a lot about mudslinging as a boy and as I grew older it was a rite of spring to get some mud and a stick and practice mudslinging. I soon learned that a mud ball that was too wet and slimy not only made a mess of my hands and clothes but also would not stay on the stick until the proper time to go flying off. A mud ball that was too dry would break into small pieces partway through the slinging process and send pieces of semi-dry mud everywhere.

It is obvious that mudslinging means something different to the politicians running for upcoming state and national offices as their TV advertisements are poorly crafted and not following mudslinging rules. A good mudslinger would never go to the manure pile for mud to sling but some of the politician's advertisements are slinging mud balls against their opponent made from something that is coming from deep in the manure pile and even smells like it.

I am sure you are beginning to get the picture so let's put a twist on mudslinging, Paulding County style. As a young boy I could tell the other boys that they didn't have the right type of mud, stick or delivery style, but if their mud ball went further into outer space as it passed over the barn, I was probably wrong. This brings up the nature of mudslinging that is the real test of character, knowledge and ability as each boy slinging mud would demonstrate to the other boys how he was able to send his mud ball the furthest. Politicians can learn something about mudslinging because if it is done right everyone benefits. My opinion is that the slimy, smelly negative advertising needs to stop immediately and in place of it politicians need to meet face to face in debates two or three times a week in various parts of Ohio to tell the people how they are going to do the job better than their opponent. The candidates would learn from each other not by slinging smelly manure but by hearing each other's ideas and responding in a public forum. This being said, if these individuals who are candidates for the high state and national offices really want our vote, maybe they should come to Paulding County and learn how things are done from some of the best mudslingers in the world.

William Sherry

Writing for the Paulding County Progress

Jessie McCague Smith

This is your life: You were born July 10, 1864 at Arthur, Ohio, Paulding County, in an old log house that stood where Mrs. Fremont McCague now lives. Your father was John McCague, Sr. You lived there with your parents and grew up to womanhood. In the year of 1886, at the age of 21 you married Thelbert Smith. To this union, three children were born: Grace Lloyd of RR1 Oakwood, with whom you now live, Guy Smith who lives with you and your daughter and Minnie Fredrick, now deceased.

Then you built your home one mile north of the Rohlf School in Defiance county and lived there 14 years. You then sold out and built a home one mile west of Arthur in 1901. Here you had to work hard as your husband was ill most of the time. You used to cut wood with the axe and buck saw, husk corn and drive a team of horses farming. Plus all this hard work, you have also devoted a lot of time to your son Guy now 61 who had been an invalid all his life.

Death has darkened your door twice, first February 6, 1934 when your husband passed away. He was a farmer and a carpenter. Next your daughter was taken by death, but you did not let this get you down. You have had a happy and prosperous life.

All of the roads in the Township were mud when you were first married. The first stone road was the Oakwood Pike, now 66, which was stoned in 1901. Your first car was a 1916 Overland. You can remember when the Arthur Church was built in 1874. You can also remember the old log church that was first across the road from the present church.

Your hobby is sewing quilt pieces and quilting. You have made over 75 quilts in your life time. You also take pride in raising a good garden and nice flowers.

Harley Shisler

Writing for the Oakwood News July 1955

Joe Snyder

Joe Snyder was the postmaster in Oakwood for 20 years from 1991 to 2011. When he came to Oakwood, Don Adams and Ed Booher were the rural mail carriers, Shelly Roughton was working as clerk and Jeanette Figert was the casual clerk, filling in as needed. Later when Shelly became postmaster at Melrose, Karen Kosch joined the staff. Joe had worked as a city mail carrier in his home town of Leipsic before coming to Oakwood.

Joe was a very kind hearted person. He really loved children. Soon after he came, the employees of the post office started the "Elf Project". They would get information about students in the local school who were probably not going to have a very nice Christmas and them put their ages and genders on an "Elf tree" at the post office. Members of the community would purchases gifts for these children. At first the post office employees would deliver the presents a few days before

Elliott Kosch, Joe Snyder and Melissa Figert

Christmas. In later years, they would invite the children to come to the post office in the evening where they would receive their gifts from

Santa Joe. Joe loved doing that and seeing the happy faces of the children as they received their gifts.

Karen Kosch

The Oakwood Mutual Telephone Company

The first meeting to organize a Mutual Telephone Company was held in Oakwood on January 19, 1905. Officers elected at that meeting were: William H. McClure, president; Elias Young, vice president; George M. Campbell, secretary; and S. S. Shisler, treasurer. The executive committee consisted of these officers plus a representative from each line. These representatives were: R. M. Weible, J. W. Whitney, J. M. Tong, Roy Asire, Charles Kirkendall, John Shock, George H. Whiting, Frank Rhees, and John Adams.

In March 1905, Mrs. J. Counsellor was hired as the first switchboard operator. She was to be paid 15 cents per month per telephone. The switchboard was located in a frame building that also served as a restaurant which Mrs. Counsellor operated. It was located near where the American Legion building is now located.

A year later, a toll line was constructed to Arthur and her wages were raised to $25.00 per month. In July of 1906, a line to Dupont was authorized. Later that year, a line to Grover Hill was authorized and in May 1907, a line to Cloverdale.

In May 1907, the telephone company leased the second story of the Wiseley store building for a period of ten years for the use of a Central office and living quarters. The rent was $4.00 per month. In July of that year, L. D. Kohler was employed as operator and general manager of the office. His wages were $30.00 per month.

Other people who served as operators during these first years were: Roy Brown, Miss Eva Wolf, Miss Ella Sullivan and Manford Hoover.

In 1914, Deak Williams was hired as operator and lineman. He kept this job for twenty years. Miss Eva Wolf was the other operator. In May of

1915, the switch board was moved to the second story of the Shisler building. In 1920, the telephone company purchased the building from the Shisler heirs for $1,000 and each subscriber was assessed $3.75 for the purchase, payable in three installments.

Other operators and linemen who served during the first 50 years of operation included: Faye Leatherman, Mrs. Alla Winner, Miss Marie Holmes, Miss Doris Timbers, Mr. and Mrs. Clint William, Mr. and Mrs. Karl Adams, Mr. and Mrs. Harry Fuller, Mr. and Mrs. Dean Lighthill, Carl Agness, Guy Carnahan, Maxine Merckel, Maxine Riley, Violet Bupp, Vera Rey Kretzinger, Erma Thomas, Mildred Young, Louise Hosler, Fairy Koch, Deltha Hillier, Betty Hanenkratt, and Lois Bidlack.

In 1934, the company was incorporated under the laws of the State of Ohio. The Board of Directors at that time were: Charles V. Thrasher, I. F. Leatherman, C. W. Cunningham, W. V. Kretzinger and E. J. Dickey.

In 1935, the Melrose Telephone Company consolidated with the Oakwood Mutual Telephone Company. Mrs. Raney had operated the Melrose switchboard for a number of years.

At one time, there were two telephone exchanges in Oakwood. The Bell Telephone Co. was here for two years. It was upstairs in the Odd Fellows Room. Marvin Fuller was hired as business manager and Ethel Fuller was the operator. They had only 20 patrons and were in business only two years.

Based on articles by Harley Shisler
Written for the Oakwood News

The Train Wreck

For those of us who lived in the Oakwood area during the 1950's one of the most memorable events was the train wreck which occurred on April 11th, 1956.

The accident occurred about 4:15 AM as the fast freight with two engines and 81 cars came through Oakwood going east. The train was hauling refrigerated meats and other food stuffs and had several cars of sheep and hogs. One tank car full of molasses overturned spilling molasses into a ditch and across the roadway.

It is thought that the accident was caused by a broken wheel or axle. Marks on the cross ties showed that the wheel was off the rails before it crossed the railroad bridge.

Nearly 1000 feet of tracks were torn up; rail cars were piled three high and broken open. Fortunately no humans were injured.

The students at the Oakwood School were allowed to walk, room by room, down to the scene of the accident to view the wreckage. The village was swamped with sightseers as word of the accident spread throughout the area. Van Wert, Defiance and Putman Counties all sent deputies to help handle the flow of traffic and the onlookers.

The Wiseley Store

Allen Newton and Electus Wiseley came to Oakwood in April 1874. In 1875, they opened a general store. They continued in business together until 1888 when Electus sold his interest to Allen who continued as a

Wiseley store, Post office and print shop before the flood of 1913

grocery store only. His store was located where the park is now. It suffered a lot of damage during the 1913 flood.

Electus then opened a dry goods store in a building on the east side of First Street, located in the area where the Risley Drug Store was later operated. That building and its contents were destroyed in the big fire

The Allen Wiseley Store after the 1913 flood
Remains of the Post Office and printing office on the left

on the night of January 5, 1899 which wiped out several businesses on the east side of First Street. The location was rebuilt in brick. Allen sold an interest in his grocery store to O. S. Ritchie and the name was changed to Wiseley and Ritchie. In 1909, he moved the stock to the location that is now the State Bank building. That building which later housed B. L. Caskey, Undertaker, O'Brian's restaurant and Spencer's restaurant burnt in a fire on April 13, 1946.

The Dam at the Wood U Drive Inn and the Stoning of Route 66

In 1954, Lester Shisler built a 125 foot long dam across the ravine north of the skating rink. The dam was 15 feet high and had a 20 foot spillway in the center to allow excess water to escape. Pershing Fohner did the work with a bulldozer. The inside of the dam was covered with 60 tons of rip rap. The lake created was about five and a half acres in size. The following letter was printed in the Oakwood News in response to an article about the Shisler dam.

"It is with much interest that I read the account of Lester's Shisler's Dam at the Wood-U-Drive-In Park. My grandfather, Caleb Shisler and his son my uncle, the late Homer (Bud) Shisler built the first dam on that location. I think it was in the year 1900. I remember it was a very hot, dry summer and they done the work with a team of horses and a slip scraper. I also remember that they made some mistakes in their plans for the overflow and the first big rain that came washed a big hole in the dam. I take from the description on the new dam that Lester Shisler is building that it will be much longer and higher than the old one was. The old one, as I remember it, was only about 10 feet high.

I also think that was the same year that the road going north from Oakwood, now route 66, was first built with crushed rock. The stone was all hauled by horses on two yard wagons, and as I remember it now, it was done on a tonnage basis and if a man, team and wagon got out early and put in a good day he could make $2.50 to $3.00 per day. As I said before, it was a very dry summer and I believe that I am safe in saying that there were dust ruts in that road 6 to 8 inches deep, and when a man and team came in at night, you could hardly tell whether he was a colored man or a white man or even tell the color of his horses. "

C. C. (Clate) Robinson, Delaware, Ohio
Writing to the Oakwood News

A refreshing break at the town pump on the northeast corner of First and Main Streets

Made in the USA
Columbia, SC
24 April 2024

34846400R00089